Parenting Adult Children

Parenting Adult Children

Real Stories of Families Turning

Challenges into Successes

Dr. Fred Schloemer

ISBN 978-1-935497-47-9

Cover design by Carly Schnur
Cover photograph of author provided courtesy of CCL Photography
Printed in Canada

To contact Dr. Fred Schloemer:
fredschloemer@aol.com
www.schloemerservices.com

PUBLISHED BY

Butler Books
P.O. Box 7311
Louisville, KY 40207
phone: (502) 897-9393
fax: (502) 897-9797
www.butlerbooks.com

To my adult children, Max and Alexis,

and my grandson, Mason.

The journey we have shared

has been the most exciting and rewarding

adventure of my lifetime,

and I look forward to future chapters

with great love and anticipation.

Table of Contents

ACKNOWLEDGEMENTS

There are so many people to whom I am indebted for their help, guidance, and support in the writing of this book.

First are the many clients who agreed to let me write about them and who also participated in the creative process, giving me their suggestions, corrections, and outright complaints when I failed to capture their truth. I never dreamed when I first envisioned this project how hard it would be for them to see their stories put into print, but I am deeply grateful to them for sticking with me through the writing experience and never flagging in their resolve to see this work go forward because (as each and every one of them *often* said), "I hope that reading about my experiences might be helpful to others."

Second is my lifelong friend, award-winning author Alanna Nash, whom I can never thank enough for encouraging and mentoring me as I worked on this project, especially as I neared completion of my first draft, and began to seriously explore publication options. Alanna, you have been a source of inspiration to me for years.

To another good friend, Marie Davis, the multi-talented cartoonist and novelist whose work is published all over the world, thank you for being my first reader and staunchest cheerleader. Your excitement about this work matched my own from the start and never faltered, even when I wondered if I would ever finish it.

To my business partner and dear friend, therapist James Stone, thank you for critiquing my work, and helping me clarify and strengthen the psychological and theological language in it, as well as for your genuine shared pleasure at seeing the work reach completion at last.

And to my own therapist, Jungian analyst Dr. Robert Cunningham, thank you for being my final reader, and giving me the support and guidance to finally send this manuscript out into the world.

Some endeavors in life "take a village" to bring to fruition. I will always be grateful to each and every one of you for being my "village" in this effort.

Sincerely,
Fred Schloemer, Ed.D., LCSW

INTRODUCTION

An old saying tells us, "Children don't come with an instruction book." We might add to that old saying, " . . . *especially* when they grow up."

There are myriad self-help books on how to parent children from birth to adolescence, but comparatively few exist on how to successfully parent children once they reach adulthood. I wouldn't dream of claiming I have all the answers to that challenge. But as a career psychotherapist, I can say that I have known and worked with countless couples and individuals who were concerned about being better parents to their adult children, and we have all learned a few good things from each other along the way.

The following case histories and resulting parenting suggestions flow from almost forty years of counseling clients of all types, but especially parents of adult children, a client group I value working with so much because I am one of them myself. These casework situations and ideas for better parenting are offered here not in the spirit of an "expert" professing some mastery of a special skill set, but rather as a fellow traveler, sharing the ongoing challenges and rewards of being a parent to two wonderful adult children, who daily remind me of another old saying: "Our children come *through* us, but they are not *of* us."

In other words, we give birth to our children and we can see the impact of our own and our spouse's gene pools in their faces, bodies, and behaviors, but they are so much more than our parental genes in terms of their unlimited spirits and possibilities. They are quite literally "boundless." And perhaps that, at the end of the day, is our biggest challenge as parents to adult children, learning how to get out of their way and let them achieve their full potential.

Author's Note

Recently several authors, including two with books on Oprah Winfrey's book list, have fabricated memoirs and autobiographies. These events have sensitized writers, readers and the publishing industry to the importance of truthfulness in the writing of non-fiction. As a result, it's important for me to clarify upfront the exact nature of the casework narratives contained in this book.

The following case scenarios are all true stories of real people, clients I have counseled in my career as a psychotherapist. In most instances, the stories are almost verbatim retellings of specific events clients have reported to me. In those instances, I have changed names and other identifying information to protect clients' privacy, but have also obtained clients' written permission to write about their experiences. In addition, in most of these cases, the clients and I have actually collaborated together on the development of their stories for this book, sharing editing and rewriting tasks as creative partners to ensure that the final product is one that they feel comfortable with.

There are a few exceptions. Three of the clients whose stories are contained here have passed away. Three others are what we refer to as "composite" cases, i.e. case scenarios based on several clients with similar issues and characteristics, wherein no one single client's actual life events are portrayed, but rather several comparable clients' stories are combined. Nonetheless, these composite cases are also very "real."

Another point that needs to be addressed for full truthfulness is the way in which client-therapist dialogues have been depicted. The dialogues from therapy sessions contained in the book are authentic re-creations of actual dialogues with clients, rather than transcripts drawn from tape recordings. Except in the exceptions noted above, the clients whose conversations have been re-created here have all read the dialogues attributed to them, and have acknowledged that my re-creation of them is accurate.

Having said all of that, I attest that the stories that fill these pages are true representations of actual clients I have known through my practice, and the interventions we have made together to change their lives for the better. I offer these case scenarios here in the hopes that by sharing them, countless other people with similar challenges will find the courage, hope, and wisdom to become better parents to their adult children.

Parenting Adult Children

CHAPTER 1

Detaching with Love: How to Stop Enabling Overly Dependent or Addicted Children

Or, "What about Bobby?"

The attractive, retired couple sitting across from me in my therapy room could have been actors in an AARP television commercial. Both had pleasant, unlined faces, silver-white hair, and poised, relaxed posture. They wore stylish, high-end sports clothes and spoke with the calm dignity that comes from reaching the age of sixty-five and surviving numerous life challenges together. Yet despite their self-assured exteriors, here the two were, talking to me, a psychotherapist.

They might have been seeking counseling over the loss of a friend, or changes in their health or income. But these common seniors' issues weren't what had brought Bob and Jenny Martin to my office that day. No, the Martins were here to discuss their forty-year-old son, Robert Junior, or "Bobby," who had just come home to live with them, again.

As a career therapist, I've had the privilege of treating people experiencing various life challenges; children with autism; men and women with AIDS; and combat veterans and domestic violence victims with post-traumatic stress disorder. But over the last ten years, a new and growing client group has emerged in my practice—parents experiencing troubled relationships with their adult children. On meeting Bob and Jenny Martin, I soon learned that the relationship with their son Bobby wasn't just "troubled," but that recently it had become life-threatening for them, as well.

Social scientists tell us that today more adult children are living with their parents than at in any time in our history since the agricultural era, when multi-generational families cohabitating under the same roof were a norm. This trend toward adult children either returning home or never leaving home in the first place is due to several *other* social trends: the changing job market, high unemployment, increased divorce rates, and an economy that has suffered both inflation and recession several times over the last twenty five years. All of these forces have caused many adult children to seek help from their parents in ways that young adults didn't have to fifty or sixty years ago.

Sixty years ago, most young parents were survivors of the Great Depression and World War II, who overcame their hardships to become one of the most affluent societies in American history. Fortunately for them, economic and social conditions following World War II supported their upward mobility. They were able to raise a generation of children, the "Baby Boomers," who were used to a high standard of living and grew up expecting to provide the same solid financial foundation for their own children.

Unfortunately for those Baby Boomers who subsequently became parents, the economic conditions under which they raised their children changed. Decades of inflation, recessions, and high unemployment have left many of these Boomers' kids, today's young adults between the ages of eighteen and forty, struggling to keep their jobs, pay their bills and try, often unsuccessfully, to avoid succumbing to massive credit card debt.

Developmental psychologists add another twist to this discussion, and one of the foremost of these experts is Dr. Jeffrey Jensen Arnett. In the past, he tells us, young adults reached full adult status by completing five essential developmental milestones, usually by the end of their twenties:

- Completing school
- Leaving home
- Becoming financially independent
- Marrying or finding a significant other
- Having children.

In numerous articles and books, Arnett argues for redefining the twenties as a distinct new developmental step, which he calls "emerging adulthood," a time for finding one's sense of purpose in life. He points out that as recently as a generation ago, most young adults did successfully complete the developmental steps described above by the time they reached the age of thirty. Now however, most young adults may not accomplish all five steps until much later in life, if at all. This lag, other social scientists argue, is as much the result of changes occurring in the young adult brain as it is the consequence of various economic and societal stressors. Considering all of this, it's safe to say that whatever the reasons, today's young adults are maturing at a slower pace, and depending on mom and dad to support them until they do reach full adulthood.

This is what had happened to Bobby Martin more than once, his parents told me. Diagnosed with Attention Deficit Disorder in grade school, Bobby had struggled to complete high school and flunked out of college. Since then, his life had become a succession of failures. After each job that ended, or girlfriend or male roommate who rejected him, he had come home to live with his parents while he tried to figure out what to do next. Eventually, Bobby began self-medicating with drugs and alcohol. Recently, his drug and alcohol abuse had escalated to the point that he was stealing money from his parents, and selling stolen goods in the community to support his habit.

One evening when Bob and Jenny confronted him, Bobby became violent and ran through the house, turning over large pieces of furniture, and eventually assaulting Jenny, trying to choke her. Bob was able to overcome Bobby then called 911 as his son ran out of the house. Shortly afterward, however, Bob began to experience chest pains and was rushed to the ER, where he learned he was having a heart attack.

"I suppose I should have seen this coming," Jenny sighed. "Bobby was always so impulsive, so intent on getting his way. As a child, he couldn't wait for anything . . . just had to have it now. If he didn't, he threw the biggest tantrums." She looked at her husband with an embarrassed smile. "Bob warned me about giving into him, but I'm afraid I didn't listen. Sometimes I feel like I've created a monster."

Bob reached out and covered her hand with his. "Now Jen, there's no sense in blaming yourself," he said. "We both raised this boy together. I'm sure I could have done all kinds of things differently too."

In his efforts to comfort his wife, Bob had revealed a key factor in their family struggles, referencing their forty-year-old son as "this boy." Bobby was indeed an under-developed male, a child in a man's body, or "man-child." To his credit, Bob recognized the futility of wallowing in guilt, and supported his wife by trying to move her beyond that counter-productive feeling. But I doubted he fully comprehended the significance of his own language.

"Did you hear what you just said?" I asked him, and he wriggled a bit in his chair.

"Did I say something wrong?" he replied.

"Not at all," I reassured him. "In fact, I think you just said something very helpful. You referred to Bobby as 'this boy,' which, in fact, he is in many ways. He can't keep a job, can't sustain a relationship with a woman or even male friends, and keeps running home to his folks, then turns on them, too, when things don't go his way. That's not the behavior of an adult male."

Bob nodded, but still seemed puzzled. "Then how is my calling him a boy so helpful?"

"The words we use convey our expectations," I explained. "If Bobby acts like a boy and we call him a boy, then we subtly enable him to remain a boy."

Jenny was on the same page right away. "But he's not really a boy," she said, turning to Bob. "He's a man, or at least he should be anyway. So, if we refer to him as a man and expect him to act like one, maybe things would be different."

Bob nodded and turned to me. "Makes sense," he said. "But how do we come to really *think* of him as a man when he doesn't *act* like one?"

"What does Bobby do well?" I asked. Bob and Jenny didn't hesitate for a moment.

"He's always been good at anything mechanical," Jenny said.

Bob chuckled. "Remember the time he took the crystal chandelier apart just to see how it all fit together?"

"How could I forget?" she laughed. "I had a big dinner party planned for that night, but he got it all back together in time for my guests."

They went on in this fashion for several minutes, recounting tales of Bobby's boyhood, and the strengths he'd exhibited as a youth. I soon learned that Bobby was artistic, sensitive, and good with small children and animals.

"So, Bobby has lots of positive traits and talents," I said. "Can you give him things to do that capitalize on his abilities and give him some sense of competence?"

They glanced at one another. "Maybe *had* lots of positive traits would be a better description now," Bob replied.

"Since the drugs and alcohol took hold, he's not done much of anything positive," Jenny explained. I nodded in recognition—the story was just all too familiar. How many times had I heard a similar tale of some bright and promising life brought to ruin by substance abuse?

But, there was still more to Bobby's downward spiral, the Martins soon informed me. He had also been a talented baseball player, excelling at pitching, and dreaming of becoming a professional. His coaches had told them he was a true prodigy.

"What happened?" I asked and watched their faces fall.

"He broke his pitching arm in a car accident soon after he started driving . . . a DUI actually," Jenny explained. "It was never the same after that."

"Funny, I'd kinda forgotten about that," Bob said. They both sat for a moment in pensive silence.

"Did he ever receive any counseling after the accident?" I asked, and they shook their heads no.

"To tell the truth, we never saw a need for it," Bob confessed.

"So, is it possible Bobby has never gotten over that loss?" I asked. "That he's as unhappy with the way his life has turned out as you are with him right now?"

They both looked at each other. "I feel sure of it," Bob said, and Jenny nodded.

A hypothesis about the Martins began to take shape for me, based on my experience that unresolved grief and loss are often core issues in families with chemical dependency problems. "What about you two?" I asked. "What's been your greatest loss?"

Jenny put her hand to her throat. "Losing him," she whispered.

"It's true," Bob said. "Ever since the drugs and alcohol took over, it's almost like he's been dead to us. When I remember that other accident when he was sixteen, I'm afraid we're going to get another call some night saying he really is dead."

Jenny looked a little nervous as she considered her next comment. "Maybe he already is," she ventured. "Maybe the little boy we fought so hard to shelter and defend *is* dead. Maybe there's somebody else inside that big hulking body of his now that we need to know? If we can just get past the drugs and alcohol first."

Bob just grunted his agreement and seemed to fight back tears.

I managed to restrain my impulse to jump up, and give them both a high five. "Now you're on your way," I said instead.

The Martins were indeed on their way, but they also still had a long way to go. They had realized how they enabled Bobby's immaturity, and seen that there was much they could do to revise their vision of him from boy to man. More importantly, they had gained some powerful insights about how their fears of losing him caused them to fall prey to his "emotional blackmail" techniques, holding them "hostage" by constantly dangling the threat of his ending his life before them.

But, Bobby still lived in the basement apartment they had provided him rent-free for years. They had pressed no charges against him for his assault on Jenny, nor had they imposed any other consequences on him. In fact, they had allowed him to return home shortly after his outburst without any discussion at all.

"He seemed so ashamed of himself," Bob explained. "We figured he'd learned his lesson."

"Besides," Jenny added. "What with Bob's heart attack and all, I can really use Bobby's help around the house now."

"And is he helping you?" I asked.

They both looked down at their hands. "Well, no," they admitted.

"But, he hasn't caused any further problems either," Jenny rationalized. I knew then that the Martin's road to a healthier relationship with their son was going to be a long, complicated journey.

Chemical dependency literature stresses the role that denial plays in preventing people from facing abuse and addiction issues, whether their own or a loved one's. Author and lecturer Claudia Black tells a tragic-comic story about herself as a teenager, entertaining a date while her drunken father lay comatose on the living room floor, wondering why her boyfriend seemed so rattled. Such was her denial of her father's drinking problems that she actually thought the boyfriend was over-reacting.

This phenomenon is what some recovery experts refer to as "delusional denial," a degree of denial that is so severe it actually takes on a delusional quality. Clearly, the Martin's willingness to take Bobby back into their home after his attack on Jenny without any consequences or discussion at all amounted to delusional denial. Just a few weeks ago, he had threatened both their lives. Now there he was, back in their basement, coming and going as he pleased without contributing anything to the family household, other than the fact that he "wasn't creating any further problems."

Another concept often dealt with in chemical dependency literature is the issue of tolerance, which is a multi-faceted phenomenon. For addicted individuals, tolerance occurs when they need more of the same substance in order to get the same high, which often indicates that their addiction is escalating. For the individual engaged in a relationship with an addict, tolerance often manifests as acceptance of inappropriate behaviors by their addicted loved one. Claudia Black was unperturbed by her father's drunkenness and wondered why her date found the situation uncomfortable, because she had developed a tolerance for her father's excessive drinking.

After years of dealing with their son's various inappropriate behaviors, Bob and Jenny Martin, too, had developed very thick skins in response to his acting out. They had come to a point where they didn't really expect responsible adult behavior from him. They were just relieved when he didn't do actual harm to them or their household. This is a very dangerous place to be for the parents of a drug or alcohol addicted child living in their home. Several times monthly, the morning news brings us stories of a murder-suicide somewhere in the nation perpetrated by addicted family members who were being housed and cared for by the very people they killed.

Clearly, the Martins were at risk of further problems, perhaps even injury or death, if they let Bobby remain in their home under the present circumstances. The question for me now became how to broach this topic with them without seeming melodramatic or making them even more anxious than they already were.

"Has Bobby ever been in any kind of substance abuse treatment?" I asked.

Jenny shook her head. "No, not really," she said. "We took him to a psychiatrist when he was having trouble in school, and that's how we learned he had ADD. But he didn't like the way the medications made him feel, so he quit taking them."

Bob's brow furrowed. "That's not exactly right," he said. "Remember that group he had to attend after the string of DUI charges he got a while back?"

"I'd forgotten," Jenny admitted. "My, how he hated that! I thought we'd never hear the end of it."

"He did cut back on his drinking for a while though," Bob added.

Here seemed to be the best entry portal I was going to get. "In my field, we believe human behavior doesn't change unless people feel some degree of discomfort with their old way of operating," I explained. "Bobby hated going to the group, but he did reduce his drinking, at least briefly. What can you do now to make him feel uncomfortable enough with the status quo to motivate him to change?"

The Martins seemed stumped. "Well, that's just the problem," Bob said in a deflated voice. "We can't control the boy . . . uh, *man* at all. He's just too big to push around."

"But you're not helpless . . . are you?" I asked.

Once again, Jenny took up the idea first. "Sometimes I get so *angry,*" she said between clenched teeth. "Walking on eggshells, afraid to make waves with him, *in my own home for heaven's sake!*"

Bob was right behind her. "I get so tired of never being able to find my tools," he fumed. "And when I do try to find out where he misplaced them, he gets so upset I end up apologizing to *him!*"

I watched them for several seconds as the impact of all that they had just vented sunk in. "Isn't it about time you took your lives back?" I asked them, and was pleased to see a determined look come into their eyes.

That was the beginning of one of the most gratifying therapy experiences I've ever had. Bob and Jenny Martin were incredibly responsive and hard-working clients, who seemed to take even the smallest suggestions to heart and run with them. By the end of our first meeting, they had recognized the need to get Bobby into treatment, and not just an outpatient group this time, but a long overdue, extended residential program.

Louisville, Kentucky, where I practice, has several strong substance abuse treatment programs. One of these, the Healing Place, is a no-frills setting that requires residents to immerse themselves in twelve step principles, while rebuilding their lives "from the ground up," socially, emotionally, and vocationally. At first, Bob and Jenny balked at the idea of their fair-haired child in a gritty urban treatment center populated by "derelicts and drunks," in their words. But, when I asked them where Bobby would be after his last bankruptcy and eviction if they weren't supporting him, they admitted the obvious truth: "He'd have no other choice but a homeless shelter," Jenny said.

"So, he would be 'a derelict and a drunk,'" I replied and watched them both wince.

"Well, yes, I guess so," Bob admitted, while Jenny just sighed.

It took some doing, but before the Martins returned to my office for their second session, they had managed to get Bobby out of their house and into the Healing Place. The chief thing that they had to come to understand was the concept of "tough love," a remarkably simple and commonsensical idea, but one which is often incredibly difficult for family members of addicts to put into effect.

Tough love tells us that enabling behaviors must end, and that health and recovery can only begin with the imposing of "natural, logical consequences" for the addict. No more "helping out" or "making excuses" or "rescuing" behaviors of any kind. If the addict gets arrested for possession of drugs or a DUI, he sits in jail. No one bails him out or pays exorbitant attorney fees to reduce the charges or lighten his time served.

Sure, it's hard for parents who love their children to watch them languish in jail. But, as I often ask them, is that harder than watching their children kill themselves daily using drugs and alcohol outside of jail? That usually gets their attention, and helps them look again at the tough love literature with a little more openness.

In the Martins' case, expressing their "tough love" for Bobby meant calling the local police department, and having an officer present while they told him he would have to leave their home, and either enter a treatment program or live in a homeless shelter;

the choice was up to him. As expected, Bobby threw a tantrum, crying, shouting, cursing, and accusing *them* of abusing *him*. But thanks to the police officer's presence, he refrained from violence, and at the officer's suggestion, eventually submitted to the idea of entering the Healing Place, even accepting a ride from the accommodating cop.

Bobby's entry into treatment proved to be a difficult time for the Martins, in some unexpected ways. What they learned, like so many other substance abusers' parents have before them, is that moving beyond an enabling relationship with an adult child is far easier said than done. Despite hating the disruption and anxiety Bobby had brought into their lives, they had to admit something about their previous dysfunctional relationship with him had met some needs for them.

"It's embarrassing to say it," Jenny told me one day after Bobby had been away several weeks. "But, I don't know what to do with myself sometimes. There used to always be some mess of his to clean up, or his laundry to do. And this is the really scary part . . . I even think a part of me misses the little adrenalin surge I got every time he blew up and caused a commotion. How sick is that?"

"Not sick at all," I was able to reassure her. Once more, chemical dependency literature gives us some helpful insights for understanding Jenny's troubled feelings as Bobby and her family moved from addiction to recovery.

Recovery literature tells us that certain roles characteristically emerge in the dysfunctional family, including victim, rescuer, scapegoat, and hero. On the up side, these roles help members of the troubled family cope with their lot, giving them a job to do and a sense of purpose in the midst of the family's emotional chaos. On the down side, these roles are prescriptive and self-limiting to the family members who play them, trapping them in a job they don't really want to do, preventing them from being fully authentic.

Like it or not, Jenny had mastered the role of rescuer to Bobby's role as victim. Against her will and better judgment, she had learned to over-function in response to Bobby's under-functioning. She had inserted herself between her husband and her son, playing mediator in their sometimes-heated, male turf battles. When Bob ranted and railed at Bobby's carelessness with his tools, Jenny went searching for the missing items in Bobby's room and restored them to Bob's toolbox, incognito. The irate men folk went their way, grumbling under their breath, and eventually forgot the incident, while Jenny lost sleep, wondering and worrying when the next family crisis was going to erupt.

Because they were such apt students of recovery concepts, and so motivated by their own pain to make changes in their lives, the Martins grasped all of these concepts readily, without the defensiveness some family members of addicts manifest when they have to come to terms with their own role in the addictive cycle. They took to heart every idea we processed in our meetings together, and went home and practiced new ways of behaving individually, in their marriage, and in their relationship with their son.

The last time I heard from the Martins was a brief phone conversation telling me that Bobby had been clean and sober for six months, was still living at the Healing Place, and was starting his own business as a handyman, "*Bob* Martin Enterprises." Recently, they reported, he had approached them and asked that they call him *Bob* rather than *Bobby* from now on. In that small gesture which had huge symbolic significance, I saw more hope for the Martin family's future than in any single other event that had occurred in our work together.

Suggestions for Further Reading and Learning

Parents interested in learning more about the ideas and problem-solving strategies shared in this chapter will find it helpful to explore some of the following readings and other resources:

Adams, J. *When Our Grown Kids Disappoint Us*. New York, NY: Free Press, 2003.

Arnett, J. J. (2010). "Oh, Grow Up! Generational Grumbling and the New Life Stage of Emerging Adulthood." *Perspectives on Psychological Science*, 5(1) 89-92.

Beattie, Melody. *Codependent No More: How to Stop Controlling Others and Start Caring for Yourself*. Center City, MN: Hazelden Foundation, 1987.

Black Claudia. *It Will Never Happen to Me: Growing Up with Addiction As Youngsters, Adolescents and Adults*. Bainbridge Island, WA: MAC Publishing, 1982.

Conyers, B. *Addict in the Family: Stories of Loss, Hope and Recovery*. Center City, MN: Hazelden, 2003.

Henig, R. M. (2010). "What Is It About 20-Somethings?" *New York Times Magazine*, August 18, 2010.

Kinney, J. *Loosening the Grip: A Handbook of Alcohol Information*. Columbus, OH: McGraw-Hill Higher Education, 2009.

York, P. & D. and Wachtel, T. *Tough Love*. Garden City, NY: Doubleday & Company, 1982.

In addition to these readings, I strongly encourage parents to attend an Al-Anon meeting, a Families Anonymous meeting, or a codependency support group meeting in their community. Finally, parents dealing with an alcoholic or drug-addicted adult child will find it helpful to visit a residential chemical dependency treatment program in their area, and consult with the staff about their child.

CHAPTER 2

Overcoming Parent–Child Enmeshment with Better Boundaries

or, "Hail, hail the gang's all here . . . ugh!"

Traditional wisdom in the study of family systems tells us that there tend to be two main types of dysfunctional families, the disengaged family and the enmeshed family. In the disengaged family, members lack close ties, going their own way and living largely separate lives. The enmeshed family is just the opposite, manifesting over-involvement in each others' lives and blurry boundaries. These are the families where, when you ask *one* member a question, all the *others* present answer for them; or where the kids tell mom and dad what to do, but take parents' directions poorly.

In my own experience, it's been hard to claim that *any* family is totally functional or dysfunctional. Rather, I've found that most families manifest some features of both states of being, depending on what's going in the family's shared life. Special stresses such as illness or joblessness may bring out the dysfunction in even a healthy family. Conversely, special positive events such as births, graduations or weddings may bring out the best in a dysfunctional family. Dora Pritchard's family was a prime example of the family that shows features of both worlds.

The Pritchards were a loving, close-knit, Irish Catholic clan who ran their own community theater troupe and public relations firm headed up by Rob, the silver-haired family patriarch. Rob may have been the creative genius behind the family's numerous professional endeavors, but his wife, Dora, was the true head of the household and heart of the family.

Despite her modest demeanor and diminutive size, Dora was a survivor of child abuse who had overcome various hardships growing up in a large family-of-origin. Her father was a hard-nosed military surgeon who had moved his wife and children across the globe numerous times during their life together. Dora and Rob first met when her dad was stationed at a large military base in Japan, where Rob was director of activities at the post's social center. The two had played roles as John and Mary Proctor in a production of Arthur Miller's *The Crucible*. Shortly after rehearsals began, Rob had whispered to a fellow cast member, "I'm going to marry that girl."

Nonetheless, Dora hadn't been so easy to win over. "I thought he was awfully handsome and very talented," she reminisced in one of our first sessions. "He sang beautifully, and played guitar in a rock band on base, but he struck me as an awful *'player'* in other ways, as well. He had a roving eye and all the girls liked him so much . . . I just figured all he was looking for was a fling and I had no interest in that."

Dora had already leveled her sights on higher ambitions; she wanted to be a teacher, even though her father had scoffed at the notion, telling her she "wasn't smart enough to make it through college." It was the kind of emotional abuse he had dished out to her and her siblings throughout their childhood, and it became the foundation for the low self-esteem and depression she struggled with throughout her life.

Dora's crushing self-doubt and depression had led her to seeking treatment with me, after a long hospitalization for what she always described as "my breakdown." This breakdown was initially triggered by her being fired from a teaching job she loved as a Catholic elementary school teacher, presumably due to her frequent absences caused by her various medical problems, but more correctly, she believed, because the principal didn't like her.

At one time, she had given up her dream of becoming a teacher after she succumbed to Rob's charms and the two eloped at age eighteen. But after years as a stay-at-home mom, she had finished her degree in education and earned her teaching certificate, all the while still fulfilling everything that was needed of her as a full-time wife and mother. This clearly was a woman who knew how to get the job done. Yet now, against her will, she was without a job, and the resulting blow to her self-esteem was devastating.

Dora's treatment focused first on alleviating her depression, largely through repairing the psychological damage brought about by her father's emotional and physical abuse. Her psychiatric diagnosis was post-traumatic stress disorder, a chronic condition common in abuse survivors, with symptoms including panic attacks, feelings of dread, and difficulties trusting others. She also suffered from several disabling medical conditions, including chronic fatigue syndrome, rheumatoid arthritis and fibromyalgia, a debilitating auto-immune system disorder.

Dora responded well to cognitive behavioral therapy

techniques, a pragmatic counseling process focused on helping clients become aware of their negative thinking and self-defeating assumptions, so that they can develop new, more effective ways of thinking and behaving. Despite her progress learning to manage her depression and anxiety, Dora soon came to terms with the saddening realization that she may never be able to work again due to the daunting combination of medical and psychiatric issues she faced.

Reluctantly, she filed for long-term disability assistance through Social Security and won it on her first attempt, a rare occurrence except in cases where it's clear the individual is gravely impaired. This outcome proved to be a bittersweet victory for Dora, and she wiped frustrated tears from her eyes as she reported on it to me in therapy. "I'm glad to know I'll have financial help for the rest of my life," she said. "But, God how I hate to think of myself as *disabled!*"

True to the survivor spirit within her, Dora soon rallied and came to enjoy the new life she led as a wife, mother, and grandmother. She supported her husband in his sometimes chaotic business, and her four grown kids in their hectic lives as students, actors in the family's theater troupe, and parents themselves. And therein lay the challenge which soon became the focus of our ongoing work together.

"I love my kids like nobody's business, *but* . . ." she began our session one day. "I never dreamed that at age fifty-five I'd still be wiping their bottoms!"

She was speaking metaphorically, of course. But the metaphor was an apt one, because in the years since her retirement, Dora's home had become both Grand Central Station and Ground Zero for the vibrant, talented tribe of busy adult children and her bohemian husband who clearly owned her heart, but also stressed her to the limit at times.

Rob always had a new public relations pitch in the works, and relied on Dora to be his ghost-writer and secretary in submitting proposals to secure contracts. Their oldest son, Rob Junior, had two pre-school daughters whom Dora loved baby-sitting, but after a long day with the toddlers, she often had to take to her bed to nurse her chronic fatigue syndrome. Oldest daughter, Aggie, struggled with depression and her own self-concept problems related to being overweight. She was prone to coming home to mom and dad's house to crash, sometimes spending days calling in sick to work and watching television on their living room couch.

The youngest kids, Doreen and Zeke, were college students who lived their lives careening between one class assignment and another, all needing mom's help, of course; or else they were memorizing lines for their next play with dad, also needing mom's help. Zeke was a true prodigy with a beautiful baritone voice and a natural gift for acting that made Dora's heart soar with pride, but also made it hard for her to say no when he came to her for help, even when she was bone-tired and needed to rest.

"Sometimes I just want to run away from home," she told me one day. "But I don't have anywhere to go."

Dora's dilemma was a poignant one indeed. Here was a woman who had overcome her history of child abuse to become a successful teacher, as well as an effective, supportive wife and mother. She had come to terms with her disabling medical conditions, and found contentment and meaning in helping her husband and kids reach for their dreams. But somewhere along the way, she had also lost her sense of *self*, a condition that many authors and therapists have identified as "codependency."

Before going another step here on the topic of codependency, I need to confess my conflicted feelings about the whole concept. The idea first originated decades ago in chemical dependency literature as the term "co-addict," referring to the particular, idiosyncratic enabling behaviors that emerge in spouses who live with alcoholics or drug addicts. The gist was that people who live with addicts begin to manifest their own dysfunctional, addict-like behaviors. While not addicted to a substance themselves, they act in many ways just like someone who is, addicted to the drama and adrenalin rush that results from living with an addict.

From there, the term morphed into the term codependency, thanks largely to the landmark work by Melody Beattie, *Codependent No More*. Over the years, countless clients have reported benefiting tremendously from this wonderful work by Beattie. I've read and reread the book myself on several occasions, and overall, I think it's one of the most important self-help books ever written. That said, I have serious issues with the whole idea of codependency as a dysfunctional condition that needs to be corrected through therapy.

While admiring Beattie greatly, my chief problem with her conceptual model is this: if you complete her diagnostic checklist of codependent traits (a checklist that goes on for several pages, by the way), you'll find that not only are *you* codependent, but *so is every other human being that has ever lived* since the dawn of time. There is a very fine line between the dysfunctional condition of codependency and the wonderful human condition of true love and devotion. Both are feeling states that involve some degree of emotional enmeshment between us and another person. The chief difference is that "true love" is an enriching and life-giving feeling state, whereas codependency is an emotionally draining and soul-sapping condition.

But, just think about your own loving relationships throughout your life and ask yourself the tough question: did you always know, day to day, whether the passionate feelings you were experiencing were "life-giving and enriching" versus "emotionally draining and soul-sapping?" My guess is probably not, because that's not the way human beings experience love. We don't evaluate and analyze when we're in the midst of it whether what we're feeling is healthy or not; it just "is what it is," and we go with the feelings, one moment and one day at a time.

Dora Pritchard had read Beattie's book and was comfortable enough with the language in it to willingly acknowledge that she had a "codependent personality" herself. "But what do I do about it now?" she asked.

The first recovery task for many codependent people is some basic training in assertiveness skills. Dora was so empathic and so nurturing that it never occurred to her she could say no when a family member asked for her help. Rather, her immediate response was to figure out some way to meet their need, no matter how much it might stress her to do so.

Dora wasn't alone in this respect. One of the most common traits I see in my clients who are struggling with parenting adult children is this misguided nurturing instinct. I'm not sure where it originated, but somehow in the last two to three decades, America's parents have embraced the wrong-headed idea that being a good parent means doing anything and everything that their children need or ask of them. Never since the dawn of humankind has there ever been a time in history when children were as indulged as they are today in modern American society. On the contrary, until relatively recently, children were considered chattel, born to serve their parents' needs and work long hours in the family's farm or other business.

Certainly that state of affairs wasn't a good thing either. But, nor is the present state of affairs, wherein children are being indulged by their parents into a state of emotional, social and financial dependency that reaches way into their young adulthood. In many ways, I believe that the best thing we can do for our children is to teach them self-sufficiency, as is appropriate for their given age and *developmental capabilities*.

Clearly a toddler can't be truly self-sufficient in any way. On the other hand, she may very well be able to cope with many things a toddler struggles with on her own if we just stand back and let her try, rather than rushing in and making life easier for her the minute she expresses some frustration or discouragement.

The same is true for our adult children. We've already noted that young adulthood is fraught with numerous developmental challenges, including finishing school, getting a job, and finding meaningful relationships. These are all steps in a journey that no young person can achieve without knuckling down, facing their issues, and doing the hard work of "suiting up and showing up" to "real life" every day of their lives.

Yet, often parents of adult children come to me and present me with some variation on these questions: "How can I help my child to succeed and overcome the hardships they're experiencing? How do I save them from the struggles they're having? How can I make their life easier?"

Some of these parents have a hard time hearing me when I suggest to them: "Maybe you don't need to."

"But my kids are my life!" They sputter. "I'd do anything I can for them! How can you be so heartless?"

My answer to these indignant parents is this: sometimes the greatest gift we can give our adult children is serving as an example of a healthy, resilient, self-reliant person ourselves, living our own lives in the best way possible, and expecting them to do the same thing. And that doesn't include constantly standing by to bail them out of life's difficulties. Just as we need to let a young child incur a few scrapes while learning to ride a bike, so do we need to let our adult children take a few lumps as they go out and face life.

Dora was not one of the indignant ones when I first posed the idea that maybe she needed to do a whole lot *less* for her family. In fact, she embraced the idea whole-heartedly. "That sounds *wonderful!*" she said. "But how do I get there?"

We started with some readings and role plays on assertiveness skills. As a college professor in a nearby school of social work, I'd often used the book, *Messages: the Communication Skills Handbook*, by McKay, Davis and Fanning. This remarkable work contains several chapters dealing with assertiveness and conflict resolution skills, which I've rewritten into handouts I give to my clients in sessions.

One of the basic ingredients in effective assertiveness is something called the "whole message," which sounds so simple on first learning about it as to seem almost silly. However, *doing* it is a whole lot harder. The basic idea is that when we use the words, "I see, I think, I feel, and I need," at the start of our communications with another person, we generally experience more positive results than we do when we start sentences with, "*You* do this or that or the other thing."

So, in Dora's case, we practiced the following "I messages:"

"Rob, you know I support your business totally, but when I stay up late at night helping you with one of your projects, I can't get out of bed the next morning. We need to find another time to do these jobs."

"Rob Jr., you know I love babysitting for the girls, but sometimes when I get home after being with them, I'm exhausted. I think we need to cut down on the hours I spend with them each week."

"Aggie, you are always welcome in our home. But you have a home of your own, too. I need you to be at your house more, making it your special safe place. Let's go shopping and figure out what we can do to make you more comfortable in your own home."

Dora rose to the challenge of learning assertiveness skills like a pro. Each week she would come in with new tales about the firmer boundaries she was setting with her family, talking excitedly about how much better she felt now that she seemed to have more control over her schedule and environment.

Dora's halcyon time of heady progress setting better boundaries with her family encountered a definite bump in the road when Aggie was diagnosed with a serious neurological disorder that caused her severe headaches and dizziness. She couldn't work or take care of herself for several weeks, and moved in with Dora and Rob to convalesce. At about the same time, Rob Junior started experiencing unexplained anxiety attacks, and called Dora daily, asking her to help talk him through them. Shortly after, Doreen came to Dora, and announced that she was pregnant and experiencing terrible morning sickness. Within just a few weeks, Dora's improving family life had come totally undone.

"I feel like I've had a total relapse," she moaned in our next session. "I was being so firm and clear with everyone and now I'm right back where I began, or *worse!*"

"Well, not exactly," I replied. "Our grown kids genuinely need us some times, and it's not being codependent when we help them at those times. It's only codependency when we jump in and help them when they could be and should be taking care of themselves."

Dora was reassured by this distinction, but still struggled with the return of her old depression during the months when her kids were so beleaguered. Nonetheless, her fierce mothering instincts fueled her determination to see her brood through this tough time and fight their way to better days.

Those came with the arrival of Doreen's baby, the family's first male grandchild, and Aggie's regaining her health sufficiently to move back into her own home. Dora reported on these events with an excited smile and loads of baby pictures one day, and I was able to give her a clean bill of health.

"It's finally gone, isn't it?" I asked. "Your old companion, depression, seems to have left the building."

She smiled broadly. "Yeah, I think so," she agreed. "Oh, who knows when it may be back? I can't seem to shake it permanently yet, but maybe some day I will."

And I think she will, too. In the meantime, in my follow-up sessions with her, I encourage Dora to continue practicing her new assertiveness skills. She's gotten very good at them, in fact, recounting in our sessions how she's stood up for herself with irritating in-laws or anyone else who tries to take advantage of her good nature and giving spirit. I always look forward to going to one of Rob's theater productions where I can catch glimpses of Dora in the wings, brandishing her clipboard, playing stage manager, herding actors and stagehands backstage, helping her family and herself to a healthier life, *mainly by taking better care of herself.*

Suggestions for Further Reading and Learning

Readers wanting to know more about the skills that helped Dora improve her life and family relationships will find the following literature helpful:

Arnett, J. J. (2010). "Oh, Grow Up! Generational Grumbling and the New Life Stage of Emerging Adulthood." *Perspectives on Psychological Science,* 5(1) 89-92.

Beattie, Melody. *Codependent No More: How to Stop Controlling Others and Start Caring for Yourself.* Center City, MN: Hazelden Foundation, 1987.

Campbell, R. and Chapman, G. *Parenting Your Adult Children: How You Can Help Them Achieve Their Full Potential.* Chicago, IL: Northfield Publishing, 1990.

McKay, M., Davis, M. and Fanning, P. *Messages: The Communication Skills Book.* Oakland, CA: New Harbinger Publications, 1995.

In addition, readers may find it helpful to attend a codependency support group in their community. They can find out where such meetings occur by calling the nearest community mental health center in their area.

CHAPTER 3

How Setting a Child Free Leads to Growth and Healing

Or, "When does my *child* become an *adult?*"

Sometimes as parents, we do all the right things, but no matter how hard we've tried, things just don't turn out the way we'd hoped. As we saw with the Martins, this is especially true for parents of children with alcohol or drug issues.

Addiction specialists tell us that the earlier a child begins abusing drugs or alcohol, the greater the damage they may experience to their neurological, psychological and social development. Some experts even believe that young people can fixate emotionally at the age they were when they first began abusing substances, making their successful entry into recovery, as well as into adult life, especially difficult to achieve. When this type of delayed development occurs, it can be particularly confusing for parents to sort through the question of when to nudge their children out of the nest to face the adult world on their own. The natural tendency is for parents to want to protect their children as long as possible. But sometimes, just by the mere fact of their turning eighteen, a child becomes accountable, at least legally, as an adult, and has to face new and harsher consequences for their substance abuse or other behavior problems.

For parents dealing with these early substance abusers, family life is often a painful, heartbreaking reality. Despite their best efforts, their child's addictive behavior becomes so deeply entrenched and so resistant to intervention that it can take near superhuman efforts for the parents to get the help their child needs, as well as the support from professionals that they, as parents, so desperately need. Unfortunately, many mental health and substance abuse professionals actually blame these parents, calling them enablers, codependents, and "the real problem" behind the child's addiction.

But as we saw in our chapter dealing with the definition of codependency, there is often a fine, ambiguous line between real love and codependency. By far, most of the behavior parents of addicted children demonstrate in parenting their children is motivated by true love and the best of intentions. Often, when the child's addiction worsens, it has nothing to do with the parents' behavior, but rather everything to do with the addictive trajectory the child is on and the child's social relations outside the home.

As a result, I consider the treatment professionals who blame parents for their child's addiction to be dead wrong. The very idea flies in the face of everything we know about addiction as a primary, progressive disease with complex genetic and psychosocial origins. It also contradicts the traditional wisdom of twelve step groups for family members of addicts such as Al-Anon, where parents struggling with guilt are often reassured with this message: "If you were powerful enough to *create* your child's problems, shouldn't you also be powerful enough to *solve* them?" At the risk of overstating the obvious, the answer is an emphatic, "*No!*"

Audrey Talbott was the classic example of a parent who did all the right things but got all the wrong outcomes, at least for a while anyway. Eventually her efforts paid off with better results and her story had, if not a happy ending, at least a "happier today." This came about mainly through her hard work and perseverance, but also through her son turning eighteen and becoming an adult in the eyes of the justice system.

I had been working with Audrey and her family on and off for four years, ever since her adolescent son Eric was expelled from the Catholic grade school he attended. Eric had admitted to playing with matches and accidentally burning down a storage shed behind the school. He had also been accused of other wrongdoing that he denied, including bullying and stealing from peers.

From the outset of Eric's problems, his parents and particularly Audrey had taken every step possible to get him the help he needed. They had had him evaluated by psychologists, psychiatrists, medical doctors, and social workers. They had hired attorneys to see that he got age-appropriate legal consequences for his behavior problems, including counseling and community service. But at every turn, Eric's behavior problems and abuse-addiction issues seemed to elude these interventions.

While struggling with his studies in middle school, Eric had been diagnosed with attention deficit disorder and started on medications. As often happens with children on drug therapy, the medication had helped increase Eric's tolerance for stimulating situations, but it had also caused him to be irritable and moody at times.

When I first met him, Eric was a handsome, bright, and likable fourteen-year-old who had a wicked sense of humor. Yet he struggled with both depression and anxiety, causing him to alternately misbehave and get into trouble, then retreat into a shell. He isolated himself in his room for days at a time, listening to heavy metal rock music and rejecting his parents' efforts to engage him in normal family life with his two younger sisters, who idolized him. The family tree included several relatives who had been diagnosed with psychiatric and chemical dependency problems, two of whom had committed suicide. Given that history, Audrey understandably feared for her son's future, and sadly her fears would prove to be on target.

As Eric neared his eighteenth birthday, his problems escalated. At the end of his senior year, he was expelled from yet another private Catholic school, one of the best high schools in the region. He was also caught shoplifting in a local supermarket and vandalizing the grounds of a posh country club adjoining his family's subdivision. Audrey correctly suspected the cause of Eric's mounting behavior problems—drug and alcohol abuse. She had found beer cans, and drug paraphernalia in his room, and had watched his behavior at home become increasingly erratic. He spent many of his nights sleepless, roaming the house, binge-eating, and leaving messes everywhere. When she found evidence that he had been falling asleep while smoking and dropping his cigarettes onto the furniture and floors, Audrey became fearful for her whole family's lives.

"He's going to burn us all up in our sleep," she predicted in my office one day.

Clearly, Eric and his folks were at the lowest ebb I had ever known them to be in my years of working with them.

34

It's been my experience with most parent couples that mothers tend to be more nurturing and supportive, while fathers tend to be more structured and firm. Audrey and Tom Talbott were no exception. Audrey always tried to take the gentler route, while Tom wanted to use tough love techniques. This resulted in a power struggle between the two that Eric gladly stepped into, playing one parent against the other to deflect from his own troubling behavior, in a dysfunctional family dynamic therapists call "triangulating." So as Eric's acting out increased, his parents became more frustrated with each other. While each struggled in their own way to quell the rising chaos in their family, no one felt effective or satisfied in their family roles.

Along the way, Audrey had rightly intuited that Eric was moving from drug abuse into full-blown addiction. Despite numerous scrapes with the law that his attorneys had always been able to rescue him from, Eric was once again breaking the law by buying drugs and alcohol; later they would learn that he had also been dealing drugs to support his growing habit. But caught up in his own denial, Eric seemed impervious to the legal risks to which he was exposing himself and his family. Like most addicts who haven't hit their bottom yet, he was riding the wave of invincibility his drugs gave him. When Eric finally did crash and burn, he did it in his usual dramatic, heart-wrenching fashion.

The weekend following his eighteenth birthday, Eric went on a new kind of binge—not food this time, but drugs and alcohol . . . every drug he could get his hands on, in fact. The previous Friday afternoon, he had talked Audrey into taking him to see a psychiatrist to obtain medication to help him manage the terrible anxiety he was feeling. The psychiatrist had prescribed him an anti-anxiety medication, the Benzodiazepam, Klonopin, which he had begun taking right away, under Audrey's strict supervision. A nurse herself, Audrey understood the risks and benefits of the Benzodiazepam drug family for people with addiction issues and she was concerned that his taking this drug might exacerbate her son's addictive behavior. She tried to talk with the psychiatrist about her concerns that day, but he essentially shut her down; he was "the doctor" after all and he didn't need anyone telling him what to do with his patient, even if it was the mother of the patient who was a career nurse herself. By the way, Eric's psychiatrist that day wasn't an addictions specialist at all; he was a board-certified child psychiatrist who was used to dealing with much younger children with far fewer substance problems than Eric. It would turn out that Audrey was right and he was wrong, but there would be no pleasure or victory for her in knowing that.

We need to talk here for a moment about the tremendous vulnerability parents of children with addictions experience. Their lives at home can be a living hell. They try their best to manage their child's problems themselves, but when they find that they can't, they reach out to professionals for help. Unfortunately when they do, they're often told by those very same professionals that they've been ineffective parents, just because they haven't been able to solve a problem that even many licensed therapists struggle with. And let me confess to the reader here, I have many colleagues who refuse to treat clients with chemical dependency problems just because of that fact; the work is often long and hard and unrewarding in the end. For treatment professionals to call these parents ineffective when so many of us have poor success rates ourselves with this population strikes me as incredibly unfair, especially when I see the guilt and shame the parents take on after being dismissed by their child's clinicians as basically useless or worse yet, even harmful to their children.

The greatest folly of this attitude among professionals is that it often leads them to ignore important input from the parents. Audrey knew in her gut, both as a registered nurse and as a parent who had been through years of problems with her son, that Klonopin was contra-indicated for him. But because she needed so desperately to have someone, anyone to believe in and trust, she accepted the psychiatrist's recommendations. It was a decision she came to regret almost immediately.

The Saturday night after he had started taking the Klonopin, Eric woke Audrey by making noise in the garage behind the family's home. She looked down from her second-floor bedroom window to see him pacing in the open doorway of the garage, muttering loud, unintelligible words, waving his arms, and darting in and out of the interior of the garage as if he was looking for something, but couldn't find it.

"For the first time in my life, I was afraid of my own son," she told me later.

Hesitant to wake her husband lest he and Eric get into an altercation that would just worsen matters, Audrey slipped into her robe and went down to the garage. Once there, she soon saw that Eric was beyond her reach.

"He was talking *crazy*," she told me. "Ranting nonsense I couldn't make heads or tails of."

Running back upstairs into Eric's room, she found the bottle of Klonopin he had stolen from her purse, and after counting the remaining tablets realized that he had overdosed on it. She also found other half-filled vials with other tablets she didn't recognize, leading her to believe he had taken a potent cocktail of various drugs. Realizing the challenge she was now up against, Audrey's trustworthy "woman's intuition" came to her aid again. She left Eric in the garage, went back into the house, and called 911 to summons police help. Then she went back upstairs to waken Tom and inform him what was going on.

"I've never felt so alone in my life," she said, remembering that night. "Tom told me it was all my fault for letting Eric take a Benzodiazepam when they're known to trigger addiction problems, even if the psychiatrist had prescribed it for him. The police came and took Eric away to the nearest psych hospital, Tom stalked off to sleep on the couch, and I spent the rest of the night crying . . . all by myself in an empty bed."

Ironically, this nightmarish evening became the beginning of better times for the Talbott family, because Eric had finally reached his "rock bottom." Something about the combination of street drugs and prescription drugs he had been abusing converged in a "perfect storm" to pitch Eric into a full-blown, drug-induced psychosis. No longer could he manipulate his way in and out of intensive outpatient programs or brief inpatient psychiatric hospitalizations for "assessment." Eric had at last reached a point where he didn't know who or where he was, mumbling wildly about the crazy things he was seeing in his drug-fueled hallucinations. He was finally in a spot where he could be hospitalized against his will due to his dangerousness to self and others. More than that, this event helped Audrey and Tom to accept the necessity to take out an EPO or emergency protective order against Eric, preventing him from coming onto their premises, and giving them the power to call the police and have him arrested if he ever tried to do so.

38

It's important for us to focus for a moment on that one development alone, the taking out of a protective order by a parent against their child. The word sounds so matter-of-fact and clinical; but doing it is a soul-wrenching thing for any parent who is forced into the action. Think of it—the child you've loved, cared for and protected his entire life can now be arrested if he crosses your threshold, all because of a petition you signed. While the circumstances leading to taking out an EPO normally fully justify the action, most parents who have to take the step still find themselves struggling with terrible feelings of doubt, guilt, and shame. Audrey felt all of these feelings and more.

"Who'd have ever imagined it?" she said with a sad smile in our next session. "That I'd actually be *glad* to say my son is in a psych hospital and now going into a halfway house for addicts!"

But she was right to be glad, because this turn of events was the beginning of a whole new life for Eric and his family. Eric finished his detoxification program at the psychiatric hospital, and was discharged to Sober Solutions. This was a new residential program in the Louisville area run by Pat McKiernan, an addictions specialist who has devoted his life to helping others find recovery and stick with it. Eric didn't enter the program willingly or easily. No, he walked through its doors angry and defiant, in a pattern that had often gotten him his way before.

But Pat McKiernan isn't a man to indulge in drama and he was totally unimpressed with Eric's defiance. Ultimately, Pat and his program literally saved Eric's life; that and the changes Audrey and Tom made in their parenting practices. On entering Pat's program, Eric had to come to grips with the facts: he could either live at Sober Solutions where he had to have a job, pay rent, cook his own meals and go to twelve step meetings; or he could go to a homeless shelter for a bed each night, and live on the streets during the day. Always a bright boy, despite his fall into drug addiction, Eric saw the wisdom of making things work at the halfway house, and soon became one of its biggest success stories, becoming a group leader and house manager within six months of entering the program.

Like all recovery stories, Eric's would have many ups and downs in the years ahead. He would relapse, lose his house manager role, and eventually fight his way back to sobriety and leadership status again. A female cousin with long-term addiction issues would die of an overdose while Eric was still at Sober Solutions, and this sad event would strengthen his motivation to avoid becoming another grim statistic himself.

I still see Audrey and Tom for follow-up sessions now and then, and continue to get glowing reports about Eric's progress. The latest good news Audrey had to report was what Eric said to her at his cousin's funeral:

"Thank you, Mom, for doing what you did, taking out that EPO and forcing me into treatment. This could have been my funeral, and if things had gone on the way they were going, it *would* have been me. I still want to come home some day. But I know that I can't yet."

An Old Testament story tells how Solomon determined the real mother of an infant whom two women claimed as their own. Summoning a guard, he instructed the man to cut the child in two and give half to each mother. When one woman protested and pleaded for him to let the other women have the child, Solomon knew she was the real mother, and awarded the child to her. Sometimes parenting our adult children comes down to the same process; we have to accept the need to *let go* of them, in order to see them live and thrive.

Recognizing Eric's special sensitivities and emotional vulnerability from his early childhood, Audrey had mothered him as fiercely and protectively as any mother lioness. She had gotten him the best treatment they could find with dozens of treatment specialists and programs. She had volunteered at his school to be more involved and accessible to him as he struggled with his studies and relationships with peers and teachers. When he exhibited behavior problems and encountered legal difficulties, she had advocated for him with principals and school counselors, and she and Tom had hired the best lawyers they could afford.

Another old saying tells us, "The road to hell is paved with good intentions," and that saying could have been written with Audrey and her family in mind. In the process of fighting for and protecting Eric, they had also inadvertently found *themselves* working harder on his recovery than *he* was, a dynamic I see frequently in families with chemically dependent children. It was no small wonder that by the time he reached his eighteenth birthday, Eric had become an entitled young man who thought he could maneuver his way out of any predicament his addiction and bad judgment had created.

One of the most loving and devoted mothers I have ever known, Audrey needed only to master one of the hardest, yet most important parenting skills of all—letting an adult child suffer the natural, logical consequences of his own choices and actions alone, as a legal adult, even if he was just eighteen.

Audrey did master that skill and is still putting it into practice, setting much more effective boundaries and limits on Eric. But she is also still grieving the fact that he can't live in their home or even visit without very strict guidelines. Nonetheless, she is also steely in her resolve to never let him live under their roof again until he has proven his recovery is real and lasting. So, like most of us human beings, she's a "work in progress" . . . and coming along very well, I think.

As of this writing, Eric is coming up soon on his one-year "birthday" as a clean and sober young man. He has a job laying carpet where he's earned the position of foreman; he's also re-earned and kept his role as house manager at Sober Solutions. He has a beautiful girlfriend who loves him deeply and who has stood beside him through all his struggles. Most importantly of all, he has a wonderful, supportive family, and a mother whom I tease sometimes by calling her "The Greatest Mother on Earth." Audrey fought with all her might, often against the odds, to get him what he needed in order to be safe and well again.

Recently, I got a sense of how far Audrey has come in her own recovery when I shared a quip with her that another one of my clients gave me: "As a parent, any day that I don't get a call from the police or an emergency room is a good day for me!" The fact that we were able to laugh together now at that idea told me that Audrey and "her guys" were well on their way to healing at last. She admits that she still wakes up at night, wondering and worrying where Eric is. But it happens less often now, she says, and when it does, she's able to go back to sleep, knowing her family is safe and their future is hopeful.

Suggestions for Further Reading and Learning

Readers who want to obtain some of the information Audrey found helpful in her recovery will find the following readings valuable:

Conyers, B. *Addict in the Family: Stories of Loss, Hope and Recovery.* Center City, MN: Hazelden, 2003.
DeVaus, D. *Letting Go.* New York, NY: Oxford Press, 1994.
Kinney, J. *Loosening the Grip: A Handbook of Alcohol Information.* Columbus, OH: McGraw-Hill Higher Education, 2009.
York, P. & D. and Wachtel, T. *Tough Love.* Garden City, NY: Doubleday & Company, 1982.

I also strongly urge parents of adult children struggling with addiction to attend an Al-Anon or Families Anonymous meeting, to visit a nearby substance-abuse treatment facility, and to consult with a licensed substance abuse or mental health professional.

CHAPTER 4

Recognizing and Managing Parental Projections on Children

Learning how to let adult children be their true selves

O f all the many, creative coping mechanisms human beings employ, projection is one of the most common and effective, in a dysfunctional way. Here's how it works, or *doesn't* work, I should say.

You're uncomfortable with some aspect of yourself, some personal behavior, trait or quirk, the side of self that depth psychologists call our "shadow." Sensitive to this issue in yourself, you zero in on it when you find it in others, and may even confront it, but as "their stuff" not your own. In this way, you discharge the discomfort the issue causes you personally and displace that discomfort onto the other person, often allowing yourself to relish some feelings of righteousness and superiority for being so much wiser and healthier.

But as Jungian analyst and author Robert Johnson points out in several of his books, we can also project what he calls "our gold," or positive aspects of ourselves onto others. One of the most common examples of this type of projection is that first rush of emotion we all experience when we find ourselves falling in love. At that heady time, we imbue our loved one with all of our best hopes, dreams and expectations, making them the recipient of our most positive wishes for ourselves, the burgeoning relationship, and our newly rosy world. Often underneath even these positive projections, there is an unconscious belief that by being loved we will be made whole, and that our problems or deficits will be "fixed" in some way.

Unfortunately, this process of putting our love object on a pedestal and *loading* the budding romance with all kinds of unrealistic perceptions and fantasies can actually sabotage the relationship, especially when we have to face the grim truth that our imagined prince or princess has some warts after all. Also, when we see that who we are inside hasn't changed, we engage in more projections, making even that disappointment the fault of others.

Parents project all kinds of emotional material, both shadow and gold onto their children. I can't begin to count the times a parent has told me over the years that they were going to do all the things with their kids that they didn't get from their parents. These parents' intentions, though grounded in good faith and sincere love for their children, are nonetheless pure projection, for the parents who express them are trying to heal their own wounds through "doing things differently and better" with their children. Well-intentioned though this sentiment may be, it still loads the parent-child dynamic with an agenda from the past, and carrying agendas into relationships is a surefire blueprint for disappointment and failure.

I can thank Angela Manning for giving me one of the most memorable casework experiences I've ever had dealing with a

46

parent learning to reel in her projections on her adult children. Angela was one of the most interesting and *interested* people I have ever met. A true "seeker," she was always reading, attending lectures or workshops, and doing retreats at health spas or spirituality centers. She seemed curious to know about everything under the sun, but especially anything having to do with spiritual matters. Part of Angela's purpose in this quest was to find healing for the incredible emotional pain she had experienced at the age of five when her mother died of cancer, after a prolonged illness that had filled most of Angela's early childhood memories with smells of sickness and feelings of dread.

"One of my earliest recollections is of sitting on the floor of my bedroom closet, hugging my knees and praying to God that if I just behaved better my mother would live. When she didn't, I knew that it had to be my fault."

Unfortunately, her mother's death was just the beginning of Angela's long, complicated journey to find healing, a journey made harder by the fact that her father was a deeply depressed and emotionally unavailable man, who was never able to nurture his motherless child. They had spent her entire childhood living with other relatives, who made it clear to her throughout her formative years that she was a burdensome visitor. None of these relatives had liked or known how to relate to children, so Angela quickly grew old beyond her years, trying to be as well-behaved and unobtrusive as possible. In the process, she had lost a piece of herself, learning to compartmentalize everything she felt, relying solely on her cognitive side, a world where "everything made rational sense, and well, if it didn't make rational sense, it didn't exist!

"Growing up with constant criticism and few positive strokes,

I came to believe that deep down I truly was unlovable. Since my intellect was my only real asset, I learned to deny all emotions. Or at least, I made the choice to not feel any painful emotions."

Thanks to her incredible intellect, she had made her way through grade school and high school with stellar grades, but had never dated, and always felt alone and isolated from her peers. Then suddenly at age eighteen, she had realized with considerable surprise that young men found her attractive and they began courting her with great ardor. It was the first time in her life that she had to come to terms with the awareness that perhaps some of her perceptions weren't realistic.

"I was like a kid in a candy shop," she reminisced with me one day in session. "I'd never had a date all through high school and then suddenly in my senior year, boys were coming to visit me and sit on the front porch all evening flirting. I didn't know what to make of it!"

This latter statement revealed another important piece of Angela's character; she had no idea whatsoever how beautiful she was. Tall and slim, she moved with a willowy grace, and had an arresting, patrician countenance—the kind of woman some other women might describe as "elegant" and a "clothes horse." Admittedly, she was hardly the typical Madison Avenue icon of beauty for that day. Perky, pug-nosed Shelley Fabares, posing as a Breck Girl on the back cover of *Seventeen Magazine* held that dubious honor and she was just the kind of teenaged girl Angela was *not!* But Angela had a dignity and poise that was far more appealing than "perky" to any young men who had any sense at all. Soon after entering college, she was engaged to the wealthy scion of a local family that owned a large and lucrative retail chain.

"I did the 'young-married thing' the best I knew how," she

recalled with me in an early session. "But I didn't have any idea what marriage and family life was really about. I had no role models, after all. It just all seemed so empty and meaningless to me. So, I eventually got out, got my law degree, and went to work supporting myself and my kids."

Angela divorced her first husband when her first two children were still small, believing that there might be somebody "better" out there who could help "fix" her. Not understanding that she was still looking for an external fix, she found someone, but that marriage failed too, due to more disillusionment and projecting of blame on her part. Two marriages and now three children later, Angela found herself at mid-life, a well-to-do attorney, making a comfortable living for herself as a single woman and mother, but wondering what it all meant. An old Peggy Lee song asks the plaintive question, "Is that all there is?" That song and lyric could have been written for and about Angela Manning.

Far from giving in to this sense of *ennui*, the question, "What else is out there?" motivated Angela to pursue her spiritual quest. Due to her incredible enthusiasm and determination, she had a rich pathway, right from the beginning. Early on, she devoured the motivational works of Wayne Dyer and Deepak Chopra, but soon moved on to other works, such as *The Seat of the Soul* by Gary Zukav, and more in the same vein by countless other authors. With each self-help book she encountered, she found a deepening understanding of her self and her history.

As her quest continued, Angela explored holistic healing practices, including herbal treatments, and "body work," a combination of massage, acupuncture, and meditation. These practices helped her to wean herself from numerous prescription drugs she was taking for everything from indigestion to muscle pain. But still she kept digging for that next answer to that next question: what is it all about? She was literally insatiable in this exploration.

Along the way, Angela tried on several occasions to share her excitement about all that she was learning with her three adult daughters. To her dismay, all three expressed total disinterest in everything she was experiencing that excited her so.

Only one of her children lived in Louisville, her oldest daughter, Roberta, who lived with her husband and two preschool-age children just blocks from Angela's own home in a comfortable East End neighborhood. The other two, Sandra and Deborah, lived in Boston and New York respectively. All were successful professionals with their own demanding careers and relationships with significant others. Angela kept in touch with them often by phone, but characterized these contacts as largely one-sided. The kids were always eager to tell her about goings-on in their lives, and Roberta especially had often relied on Angela's help with baby-sitting or picking her kids up at school when they were sick and she couldn't leave work.

Angela had retired by now and was able to help Roberta on these occasions, but sometimes felt "used" nonetheless, especially when Roberta never expressed the slightest interest in hearing about what was going on in her life. Sandra and Deborah were a tad more responsive, at least asking polite questions when Angela shared her excitement about something new she was reading or experiencing. But even with them, Angela sensed a core disinterest, or at least confusion about why it was that she was pursuing this spiritual exploration.

"Why not just take up golf?" Sandra had asked her at one point.

"Why are you still seeing that therapist after all these years?" Roberta had asked her on another occasion. Angela intuited, and rightly so, that her children thought she was wasting her time and money, or perhaps even being taken advantage of by the various mentors and healers in her life. Only Deborah, the youngest, seemed to "get it" to some extent, but even she was far away and unable to provide much support to Angela.

"I suppose I've reaped what I sowed," Angela sighed to me one day. "I don't think I was ever really *'there'* for my kids, emotionally anyway. Oh, I think I did a fair job of keeping them clean, well-fed, and healthy over the years. But I never had any real interest in doing all the 'mom' things that their peers got from their mothers. I wasn't one to bake cookies for after-school treats or run them around to ball games and piano lessons."

"But how could you have known how to do all of that?" I asked. "When you never got an ounce of nurturing yourself growing up and were always made to feel like you were an unwelcome burden wherever you lived?"

Always the hard-nosed pragmatist, Angela needed to be accountable for her mistakes now, not rely on excuses. "I had a best friend in high school whose home I went to every day after school. Her mother would have a plate of fresh-baked cookies out on the kitchen table when we came in the door, and we would sit there together for hours some times, answering her questions about how our day had gone. She was always so interested and receptive to our stories, no matter how trivial or mundane they might have been, and so affirming of anything positive we had done. Oh, how I wished she could have been my mother! I could have done the same things for my kids, but I never did. And now I'm paying the price."

And herein lay the "crux of the matter" that became the focus of our work together on changing Angela's parenting of her adult children. Angela had done the best that she could for her children, raising them well, paying their way through college, teaching them by her example to be successful, independent young people. She had also worked hard to keep communication and some degree of emotional closeness alive with them. Especially considering the emotional deprivation she had experienced in her own upbringing, I believed, and told her so, that she had done extremely well as a parent—certainly far better than many parents I have known through the years.

But like all parents, Angela had also fallen into the common trap of projecting a great deal of her own issues onto her children. This isn't a mistake or error per se so much as it is mere human nature. Angela was able to articulate very well how projection had always functioned in her life and relationships. "Since my shadow self believed I wasn't loved, to support that belief I projected it outward, assuming everything negative I encountered was about me."

Never having been nurtured or affirmed by the adults in her childhood, Angela had raised her own children very differently indeed. She had provided the best for them in terms of creature comforts and education, and had continued to reach out to them through the years after they became adults. But by her own admission, she had also been emotionally unavailable to them. How could she be anything else when she couldn't acknowledge her feeling side at all for much of her adult life? Unconsciously, she had also experienced some degree of role reversal with her children over time, as she increasingly looked to them to validate the new learning and lifestyle which excited her so much. When they failed to share or appreciate her excitement, she was hurt and angry, in much the same way she had been hurt and angry as a child when the adults in her life failed to appreciate her good grades and behavior.

So much of our experience as human beings is based on our values, history, and perceptions. We respond to new experiences based on our old experiences. But therein lies a problem: not everything that we've experienced *before* really illuminates or informs what we are experiencing *now*, or *will* experience in the future. In fact, just the opposite can be true: perception is a mirror and everything we've experienced before can actually color and distort what we experience in the now and in the future. Biases based on past experiences can cause us to pre-judge, and sometimes distrust and devalue new experiences. So, past learning isn't always the best determinant of new learning. In fact, past experience can disable and disadvantage us in responding to new realities.

To break the hold her past had on her, Angela found special help "learning that there was nothing the matter with me" from two sources, an international group healing program called Landmark Education, and the book, *A Course in Miracles*. Through utilizing both of these resources, she mastered the self-awareness and self-talk processes needed to start "reeling in projections." As she often says to me in describing her ongoing work in this area, "the process is remarkably *simple*, but far from *easy*."

It begins with realizing when a projection is occurring, usually recognizable by strong feelings of anger, hurt, or disappointment with another person. Caught in the grips of a projection, we tend to assume motives or engage in "mind-reading" concerning the other person's thoughts, feelings, or intentions toward us. Once we can recognize we're in the grips of a projection, we can talk ourselves down from its ledge with some basic cognitive behavioral therapy (CBT) techniques, including:

- Sorting facts from assumptions;
- Acknowledging *mistaken* assumptions and *faulty thinking*;
- Recognizing the self-defeating thoughts, feelings, and behaviors which result from mistaken assumptions or faulty thinking; and
- Developing more effective thinking, feeling, and behavior patterns.

For most clients, the hardest part of this process is the second step, acknowledging that their assumptions are mistaken and their thinking is faulty; also that these assumptions are about themselves, not the other person. Many, if not most people, like to believe that their perceptions are accurate and have difficulty admitting otherwise. If we can't believe that our view of things is realistic and our judgment is sound, the world becomes a much scarier place to be. On the other hand, if we're having problems with any aspect of our lives, we'll never be able to change things for the better if we can't acknowledge how our own false beliefs feed into the problems.

In Angela's case, the above guidelines helped her to process her hurt feelings or anger with her kids with new ways of thinking about what was actually happening in her interactions with them. Once she could redefine what had occurred in her interactions with them, she could also re-program her old, dysfunctional ways of responding to them. For starters, she learned to practice the following mantra any time she felt negative feelings surfacing toward her children and the way they were treating her: "I made it up. It isn't true."

This mantra may seem a bit Quixotic, but it's a very effective tool for deconstructing any self-defeating perceptions that may be coloring our responses to others in our world. This philosophy also helps us realize that others are experiencing their own stuff and much of that isn't about us. Angela's new mantra for disengaging from old patterns of perceiving and responding proved to be a powerful tool: "I made it up. It isn't true." The strange, contradictory message: "I imagined all of this and it really isn't real," helped her to disengage from old anger and resentments, and to free herself from the stranglehold these negative feelings had on her heart.

A recent session revealed the extent to which Angela had overcome her old "demons." She opened the hour by talking about an invitation she had extended to her daughter Roberta to spend a day together doing lunch and taking in a new Broadway series play, *Wicked*. The tickets were extremely expensive and Angela had enjoyed the play tremendously when she saw it in New York years before. She envisioned a wonderful day with Roberta, relaxing over lunch, and watching the play together afterward, ending the experience with cocktails at the theater bar, and going their own ways after a long, wonderful "mother-daughter bonding day." But sometimes the best-laid plans go awry.

"I don't know what happened, but Roberta was in a terrible mood, and incredibly critical of me all day long," Angela shared with me in session after that weekend. "She criticized everything I did or said all that day, and seemed to be totally miserable."

Time was when Angela would have processed such an event for weeks in our sessions, dissecting every word and every nuance of the experience and trying to decide how to respond to it. But this time, Angela was able to reframe the event, instead of ruminating on how disappointed and hurt she was over Roberta's failure to deliver the wonderful day they were *supposed* to have had together.

"I don't need to know what was wrong with Roberta that day, but it was clearly her stuff, not mine. I forgive her for the hurtful things she said and I forgive myself for having had unrealistic expectations for the day."

An old cigarette advertisement coined a phrase which became a common idiom in pop culture for years afterward: "You've come a *long way*, baby!" Angela Manning had indeed come a long way, from the scared, abandoned child who felt so unloved by others in her world that she struggled for most of the rest of her life to love herself, and to trust the love of others, especially her adult children. But by working on her own issues, rather than trying to coerce or force her children to work on theirs, she was able to come to a whole new way of relating to her children, a way that worked far better, both for them and for her.

Suggestions for Further Reading and Learning

To explore some of the concepts Angela Manning found so valuable, readers will find the following resources helpful. In addition, readers can find out more about the Landmark program by going to its website, www.Landmark.com.

Adams, J. *When Our Grown Kids Disappoint Us*. New York, NY: Free Press, 2003.

Johnson, Robert. *Owning Your Own Shadow: Understanding the Dark Side of the Psyche*. San Francisco, CA: HarperCollins, 1991.

McKay, M., Davis, M. and Fanning, P. *Thoughts & Feelings: Taking Control of Your Moods and Your Life*. Oakland, CA: New Harbinger Publications, 2007.

Vaughan, F. and Walsh, R. *Gifts from a Course in Miracles*. New York, NY: Penguin Putnam Inc., 1983.

CHAPTER 5

Surviving Estrangement and Loving From Afar

When our adult children cut us out of their lives

One of the most heartbreaking things any parent can experience is the loss of a child. Yet parents often lose their children one way or another in our culture, usually through the death of a child, or an ugly divorce and custody battle. These losses call on parents to do some very challenging grief work. Nothing can ever replace the lost child, but when parents are lucky, they eventually work through their loss and rebuild their lives from there. This grieving process is a lot more complicated and difficult when a child makes a voluntary choice to remove themselves from their parents' lives, especially when the parents don't understand why.

Occasionally I encounter parents who are experiencing a total estrangement from their adult children through no apparent fault of their own. These situations always touch me as especially poignant and challenging because the parents feel so abandoned and betrayed, yet have so little information to help them work through their feelings. Thankfully, many of these clients have found ways to overcome these periods of alienation, reunite with their children, and in hindsight, be able to look back on the separation as a time the children needed to experience in order to individuate and become truly independent adults. But unfortunately, others haven't reached this positive resolution. With them, our work has had to focus on coming to terms with the loss of a child, not through an accident, death or illness, but through the child's conscious choice to cut their parents out of their lives completely, often for reasons the parent never fully comprehends.

So many experts have addressed issues of grief and loss over the years that I wouldn't dream of trumping their collective wisdom. But there is little in the literature to help parents deal with loss when it's an *imposed* separation brought about by a child's intentions to sever ties, particularly when the reasons aren't clear. While it's never easy to lose a loved one, at least in those situations when we know the person left us through no fault of their own, we can find comfort in the fact that they left us unwillingly. Everyone dies, somehow, someday, and while we miss them when they do, we know at these times that we're dealing with the mandates of the life cycle. No one lives forever.

But when someone, especially a child we love dearly, literally disappears from our life for little or no reason, the loss is magnified in many ways. All kinds of questions plague us:

- Why are they doing this?
- How can they be so cruel?
- What did I do wrong?
- How can I get them back in my life?
- Who can I turn to for help?
- How do I handle my anger and grief?
- What can I do to avoid making things even worse?

Christy and Elliot Durham were the classic "poster children" for this painful dilemma. They were a handsome, affluent, middle-aged couple, and through hard work and determination they had built a large and lucrative landscaping business from a small gardening center Elliot ran with his brother before he met Christy. But Christy had a way of getting things done and when she and Elliot first met, fell in love, and threw in their chips together, it was the beginning of a true family dynasty.

Elliot and his brother, and later his sons, were master landscape artists who created beautiful gardens for wealthy homeowners in the East End neighborhoods of Louisville. Many of their projects had won awards and they were some of the most respected landscapers in the region. But Christy had been the driving marketing force behind her menfolk's success. Her skills at connecting with people had kept their business alive through several recessions and other times of financial hardship.

For the most part, the Duncans had been just as successful in their family life. They had raised three bright, talented children; two sons, Adam and Avery, and their youngest, daughter Kelly. While the Duncans and their kids struggled with all the normal developmental challenges any family experiences, over time some very positive developments had also occurred. Both of the boys had joined Elliot in his business and had become skilled master planners in their own right. Elliot was able to semi-retire and shift into the role of a senior consultant to his sons, freeing Christy and himself to travel, a dream they had always cherished, but had never been able to act on before. Adam and his wife produced two grandchildren, both boys, whom Christy adored and who gave her life a whole new meaning and purpose. She babysat for the boys as often as she could.

Always a bit of a loner, Kelly had chosen a different path, majoring in theater in college, although she never finished her degree. Still, she was able to pursue a life on the stage and even achieved some critical acclaim for her performances in local community theater. Unfortunately, for many regional theater players, critical acclaim doesn't always translate into financial success—in fact, seldom so. Most such actors make a scant living waiting tables or teaching voice and music lessons on the side, trying to support the art they love but can't make a living at, despite their passion for it.

This was Kelly's story, and while she was clearly a bright, personable individual, Christy worried constantly about her youngest child. Sometimes Christy couldn't keep her fears for Kelly to herself, and openly aired her worries that the girl needed to develop some more gainful means of employment soon or, "she would have to come home to live with her parents forever."

Though Christy never meant these comments in a hurtful way, Kelly heard her mom's concerns for her as "put downs," and the longer they went on, the more Kelly pulled away from her mom and family. The situation reached a tipping point when Kelly suddenly pulled up stakes and moved . . . to Seattle, Washington. Despite not having a job or any significant social connections there, Kelly had preferred to move across the country rather than live closer to her family.

"About as far as the kid could go to distance herself from us, wouldn't you say?" Christy vented to me. I had to agree; it was hard to see Kelly's choice to move so far away as anything *but* an effort to separate herself from her family. That said, in an unexpected paradox, once Kelly had moved, there seemed to be a new dynamic in her relationship with her family.

Perhaps it was proof of the old saying "absence makes the heart grown fonder," but once Kelly was ensconced in her new life in Seattle, she called and wrote her family frequently, always sounding warm and loving in these communications. As a result, having been lulled into a false sense of security, Christy was all the more confused and devastated when Kelly suddenly disappeared completely from the family's radar, failing to return their phone calls or letters for weeks and eventually months on end. She even changed her cell phone number, sending a clear message to the folks back home that she wanted to have nothing more to do with any of them.

"It's like she's vanished without a trace!" Christy moaned into a handful of Kleenex. "I don't know what to do . . . put in a missing person's report with the Seattle police, hire a private detective, go out there and try to track her down on my own, or *what?*"

As the months without contact from Kelly dragged on, Christy eventually decided that it probably would be a good idea to hire a private detective. However, the outcome of that decision just made matters even more painful for her, when she heard back from the detective that he had located Kelly and she was doing just fine.

"Just fine," Christy repeated with a stunned, numb face. "Just fine . . . now that she's cut us out of her life."

Christy may have looked stunned and numb at the time, but her outer appearance belied the incredible emotional pain and anguish she felt in those days and for months, even years to come. Always a survivor, with some considerable family-of-origin wounds of her own, she had learned to make the most out of whatever life delivered to her, and forge on without complaining. Nonetheless, that didn't mean she didn't suffer considerably.

"I'm talking about the kind of grief where you're lying on the floor, crying and screaming," she said as she described those days to me.

As her therapist, I found myself feeling just as blocked and helpless as Christy did. What can any of us do when someone decides to break ties with us, especially an adult child? We can't force our will upon them or *make* them do our bidding. They're adults, after all, and have the right to live their lives the way they see fit, even if it means doing so without us.

It seems that old platitudes really do have true value sometimes. The one that came to mind for me working with Christy on the loss of her daughter was this: "If you love something, set it free. If it's yours, it will come back again. If it doesn't come back, it never was yours to begin with."

As parents, we don't "own" our children, no matter what their age. They're a *gift* from God or whatever higher power we may believe in, but they are not our *possessions*. But, as Christy pointed out to me when I shared this old saying with her, in some ways parents do "own" their children, at least for the first eighteen or so years of their lives, meaning that parents feel a strong sense of commitment to and responsibility for their children until they reach adulthood, and maybe even after that.

"I know she's her own person now," Christy sighed. "But she was my daughter for eighteen years and now I find that I can't let this thing go without one more try. I'm going to write to her and hope she finds it in her heart to read what I send her. After that, if she still decides to keep this wall up, at least then I'll know I did everything I could to try to get her back in our lives. If that's the outcome, I don't think I'll ever get closure. But at least I'll know I gave it my best shot."

As often happens in therapy, the best decisions are always the ones clients make on their own. Before our next session, Christy had drafted a powerful and poignant letter to Kelly. She brought it in to review with me in our next session and I didn't have a single change to suggest. We found ourselves sharing the box of Kleenex this time, as the letter was a true masterpiece of parental love and devotion. In it, she recounted to her daughter the many memories she cherished about her only girl's first few years, anecdotes about Kelly's emerging spirit and feistiness, even from an early age.

Christy went on to praise Kelly for her independence and individuality, always marching to a different drummer and doing her own thing, even when it meant taking a lonelier path than her classmates, who worried only about being popular and accepted by their peers. Finally, she ended with a frank and vulnerable plea to Kelly to let them all back into her life and end this mysterious and perplexing separation, if not for herself, then for the grandkids who worshiped their Aunt Kelly and talked about her all the time still, even though they hadn't heard from her or seen her for months.

I had a hard time keeping my own emotions in check as I listened to Christy read the closing lines of her letter: "Your loving mother, now and forever, no matter what happens from here."

Christy ended that session telling me she planned to email the letter to Kelly because she anticipated her daughter wouldn't sign for it or open it if she sent it by certified or regular mail. A few weeks later, I got a phone call from her saying: "Nothing, absolutely nothing . . . at least, not so far anyway." She could never let herself completely give up hoping.

So, now we all knew the awful truth at last. Through her unresponsiveness, Kelly had made her position clear: for now at least, she wanted nothing more to do with her family, even the blameless and loving nephews who adored and looked up to her. Christy would never give up the hope that someday that may change, although in many ways the continual hoping just made the ongoing separation from Kelly harder.

I continued to see Christy now and then in the months to come, as she processed her ongoing feelings about losing Kelly in such a senseless and perplexing way. Finally she ended a last session with me: "I think we've beaten this dead horse about all we can, Doc." The wry smile on her face belied the terrible grief she still carried. Christy was another survivor who wasn't going to let all the negative things in her life that she couldn't control keep her from enjoying all of the many blessings in her life that she cherished so much. But, in a recent phone conversation with me, she shared once more how much she still suffered and struggled with the inexplicable loss of her only daughter. "It's a pain that never ends," she said. "And being brave and going on with life doesn't mitigate the loss."

I was reminded by her words of something that an old clinical supervisor and mentor of mine used to repeat: "Life isn't easy on the strong. Because they handle adversity so well, everyone thinks they'll come out just fine, no matter what. So while the weak get all kinds of support with their burdens, the strong are left to carry theirs alone."

Christy was one of those strong people whose emotional pain others might not fully see or appreciate. Certainly, she had

Elliot and her other children and grandchildren to support her in grieving the loss of Kelly. But just as a mother's relationship with a child has a special emotional power, so does a mother's grief for a lost child. As a result, I'm not sure anyone else in the family or even I myself could really empathize completely or understand exactly what Christy went through in losing Kelly. "It just defies description," she summed it up to me one day.

The fact that Christy carried much of the emotional pain that Kelly's disappearance had created for the family doesn't mean that other family members didn't experience their own personal grief and sorrow. It's just that mothers are often the "feelings managers" for their families, naming and confronting the sometimes oblique emotional material rumbling about under the surface in the family's life. Men are notorious for suppressing and compartmentalizing their feelings: "Who me, go to therapy? Heck, no. I'm doing fine, thanks." But Elliott suffered in his own, albeit *different* way as a result of Kelly's disappearance. While he never sought therapy for his struggles, he definitely had some very painful times nonetheless, some of which came to light as he and Christy worked together with me on the writing of this chapter. The lesson that I think emerged for all of us in that process was a reminder that grief is a very personal and individualistic experience. The fact that someone doesn't *appear* to be deeply affected doesn't really mean very much at all in the final analysis.

Christy and I still exchange Christmas cards and have an occasional phone conversation. In those contacts, I always hear from her that Kelly has never resumed contact with her family, but that Christy hasn't entirely given up hope, at least not yet anyway.

And this, at the day's end, is the chief lesson courageous Christy Duncan imparts to us: we can love our children deeply and do everything imaginable to help them on their way in life. But all of that love and devotion can't *ensure* a happy relationship with them. Life throws us, and them, all kinds of "curve balls." Sometimes unforeseen and unexplainable life events tear us apart from our adult children. And when that happens, perhaps the best thing we can do is to leave the door open to them should they ever choose to reconnect with us . . . and all the while, continue loving them from afar.

Suggestions for Further Reading and Learning

To learn more about the healing steps Christy Duncan took to deal with her grief, readers will find the following readings helpful:

Adams, J. *When Our Grown Kids Disappoint Us.* New York, NY: Free Press, 2003.

Coleman, J. *When Parents Hurt: Compassionate Strategies When You and Your Grown Child Don't Get Along.* New York, NY: HarperCollins, 2007.

Davis, L. *I Thought We'd Never Speak Again: The Road from Estrangement to Reconciliation.* New York, NY: HarperCollins Publishers, 2002.

DeVaus, D. *Letting Go.* New York, NY: Oxford Press, 1994.

I would also encourage parents who have lost touch with an adult child through estrangement to attend a grief support group such as Compassionate Friends. While they will almost certainly find that all the other parents present have lost a child through a death, the support they find for working through their grief there will be the same; loss is loss, no matter how it happens.

CHAPTER 6

Parenting Physically or Developmentally Challenged Adult Children

When a Child Can't Grow Up

Learning that a child is physically or developmentally challenged calls on parents to make myriad life-altering decisions and accommodations. For these parents, family life reminds them daily that their children will never grow to full adulthood, but rather will always experience some degree of dependency on their parents and others. Conversely, some of the most loving and devoted parents I've ever worked with are those with a disabled child, who have spent the child's entire lifetime making sure the child never felt "less than" or marginalized in any way.

For these admirable people, day-to-day parenting calls upon them to show tremendous courage, determination, and creativity. They have to stubbornly refuse to let their children's disabilities prevent them from having a meaningful life, often fighting with schools, social service providers, and health care professionals to make sure their children's needs are met. They have to behave as if their child is just like everyone else as they go out into the world with the child, often encountering hurtful comments and stares from strangers. They have to constantly put their child first, deferring their own needs until they know that their child is taken care of, a dilemma all parents of all children experience to some extent. However, parents of non-disabled children know that their situation will change one day; their child will mature and become self-reliant, so they can look forward to a better future. That will never be the case for parents of disabled adult children. On the contrary, these parents can generally look forward to a worsening of their parenting burdens, as many disabled children's conditions deteriorate as they age; or the parents may face an even harder outcome, the early death of their child, because many disabled children have shortened life spans.

As a result, I've found that behind closed doors, many of these parents continue to grieve the loss of a more typical family life, even as they stay the course, ensuring their children have the fullest life possible in light of their circumstances. Striving to make sure that their child's world is stable and secure, these parents frequently prefer that no one see their pain, and wear a brave mask. While noble and well-intentioned, this mask-wearing can also impose a certain degree of social pressure and isolation on the parents. It's seldom a good thing for the spirit when we feel that we can't be honest about who we really are and what we really feel. Just as we saw in earlier chapters dealing with chemical dependency issues, any time one's role in the family becomes prescriptive or controlling, the family member playing that role loses a part of themselves. And that is the dynamic I worry about most in my work with parents of physically or developmentally challenged adult children.

Emily Hernandez and Chad Curtis were exactly that kind of parents . . . loving, protective, totally committed to their disabled daughter; yet also hurting deeply inside, and struggling with how to be honest about all that they felt. A bright, multi-talented, and attractive couple in their early forties, they had devoted their entire marriage and family life to one goal: keeping their daughter Maria alive and healthy. Maria coped with multiple, debilitating challenges. She was profoundly mentally retarded, with the intellectual and emotional age equivalency of a six-month-old; she was also mute and visually impaired. It took Emily fighting the "system" to get treatment providers to hear her and acknowledge the full extent of Maria's impairments, so that she could get the special services she needed.

As if all of this wasn't enough, Maria also had chronic respiratory disease, which made her vulnerable to frequent infections, and a degenerative spinal condition which left her with no strength in her torso and unable to sit up on her own. As a result, she was bed-ridden and wheelchair-bound all of her life, necessitating special skin care to prevent bed-sores.

Lest we look only at the hardships young Maria and her brave parents faced, it's important to note some true miracles which also occurred in her short life span, miracles brought about largely due to the special efforts and gutsiness of her parents.

"When she was born, they told us she'd only live to be three to six years old," Emily mused in our first session. "Well, she's made to twenty-five so far, and I'm damned proud of her for that. My girl's a real fighter."

Chad reached out and took her hand. "And who else is a real fighter?" he asked with a small smile.

"I'm busted," Emily laughed. "What can I say? After all, I'm Cuban! We love, we laugh, we fight, we cry, then we all make up and have a great meal together! But it's all been worth it when it comes to my girl. I'll fight every one of those fights again, if I have to. The only thing that matters in the whole wide world to me is that Maria gets what she needs."

As it turned out, we would all look back soon and see some important foreshadowing in Emily's comments that day. Strangely enough, Maria's needs weren't what had brought Emily and Chad in to see me in the first place. They had come in originally to rebuild their trust and closeness after Emily had engaged in an online relationship with an old boyfriend she knew long before she and Chad got together. This is yet another new phenomenon I see in my work with clients over the last ten years, since the dawn of the Internet and social networking sites.

While nothing beyond chatting had ever happened between Emily and the old boyfriend, Chad understandably felt threatened and afraid about "what might have been," questioning why Emily would need to seek the attention of another man at all, even if it was just through messages on Facebook. In our first session, I could see without a doubt that Emily and Chad loved one another deeply. But some serious damage had been done to their relationship, and it was going to take some time and some special efforts to repair it.

On first glance, this unexpected lapse in Emily's normally "super-responsible" role of wife and mother seemed a total anomaly. As she and Chad had said themselves, she was the fighter, protector, nurturer, and help-mate. Emily had changed Maria's diapers and bedclothes, fed her, and sung her favorite songs to her for the last twenty-five years. Flirting with an old boyfriend online was just completely out of character for this woman who had dedicated her life to her husband and daughter.

Or was it? Once more, a Jungian frame-of-reference gives us an understanding of the "shadow" in all of us and helps to illuminate Emily and Chad's difficult world. By her self-description, Emily was a passionate Latina, who loved life in all its facets . . . good times, good friends, and good food shared with loved ones. But, all of us have a tipping point, that place in our lives when some critical mass occurs and we can't imagine going on anymore without some change in the status quo.

Emily's love for Maria and Chad was undeniable; it had been tested and proven countless times over the twenty-five years they had managed to keep Maria alive and well, despite the overwhelming odds. But despite his love for Emily and Maria, Chad, a much more quiet and inhibited man, had dealt with his own pain by pulling away, finding solace in his work as a potter, a deeply satisfying but also largely solitary pursuit. The more Chad pulled away, the lonelier Emily felt.

Emily loved Chad and Maria unconditionally. But somewhere along the way, in the process of loving and worrying about them, she had lost track of what her own life was about. Once, she had been a talented and successful actress, theater coach, and playwright. Since the start of the latest recession, funding for the kind of projects she specialized in had dwindled, and she had found herself mainly unemployed, questioning where her professional life was going. Given all of these empty spots in Emily's heart, it was small wonder that a little special attention from an old boyfriend would at least pique her curiosity and tempt her to begin a dialogue with him.

"I had no intention of ever actually seeing him, or doing anything more than just talking with him," she swore in our initial session. While I believed her totally, it was also obvious that, while Chad wanted to, he was having a hard time doing so.

"But why even do *that*?" was his question in response, and he had a good point. If people are really happy in their marriages and love their spouses completely, why would they need to go outside the marriage to find fulfillment of any kind?

Jumping in here, I was able to give them both a quick, crash course in the concept of the shadow, and both seemed to think it applied to their situation. Though they would need to continue to work on overcoming the damage Emily's online flirtation had caused, reframing what had happened as an understandable response to the many stresses they were under, as well as the many unmet needs in their marriage, helped Emily and Chad to begin the process of healing their wounded relationship. They recommitted themselves to spending their lives together, and to making their home the safe, stable, and secure place it had been for the last two decades. However, some unexpected new wounds to Emily's heart were about to occur, and this time they would be physical rather than emotional or spiritual.

Coming down with what she thought was "a bad case of the flu," Emily found that her recovery just didn't match what she'd experienced in the past with other bouts of the virus. She remained unusually tired, listless, and even lethargic for weeks afterward, noticing after a while that her pulse and blood pressure seemed erratic. Finally one night, she experienced chest pains and had so much trouble breathing that Chad had to call an ambulance to rush her to the hospital. There, after several days of testing and observation, her physicians delivered perhaps the biggest blow of her lifetime: Emily had contracted a virus which had attacked the muscles of her heart, and it was functioning at only ten percent of normal capacity. Suddenly, in one fell swoop, she was even more at risk of dying than the physically and developmentally challenged child that she and Chad had spent their entire marriage working to keep alive.

"You know it's funny," she shared with me in a wistful way one day. "We've spent so much love, energy, and time over the years focused on keeping Maria well. Then a virus steals my health away from me just like that, almost overnight. Who would have ever seen that one coming?"

Like many parents of disabled adult children, Emily and Chad had always feared the possibility that something could happen to them that might keep them from caring for Maria. In preparation for that possibility, they had put Maria's name on a waiting list for a local, long-term care facility that specialized in treating severely physically and developmentally disabled adults. They never expected to need that placement for Maria for years to come. Now all of a sudden, they found themselves at that turning point they had hoped would never happen, not through changes in Maria's health, but in Emily's. When Emily's doctors learned about her home situation they were adamant; if she tried to continue caring for Maria, she would virtually be committing suicide.

Certainly Chad could pick up some of the slack for Emily in taking care of Maria, and had already done so. But their former family circumstances would never be the same again. It was just not going to be feasible for Maria to remain in their home anymore.

Whether through blind luck, serendipity, or divine intervention, the facility where they had Maria's name on a waiting list contacted them at about that time saying that they had an opening; would they want to have Maria enter the program now? Thus began some of the darkest hours and most difficult decision-making yet for Emily and Chad. Did they want Maria to go into this facility now? No, of course they didn't. But did they need her to enter it now, both for her own and Emily's well-being? Yes, of course they did.

This dilemma is one of the most common and heart-breaking ones I see in my work with parents of adult children with disabilities. In the natural order of things, we all expect our children to outlive us and even expect a time when our roles may reverse with them, such that they become our caregivers. However, for parents of disabled adult children, the child will never be able to take care of the parent, but rather will always be dependent on the parents' care. For these families, when parents' health begins to fail, troubling decisions need to be made about finding alternative care for the child.

To their credit, Emily and Chad had done their homework and lined up alternative care for Maria once they were unable to minister to her needs themselves. What they hadn't and couldn't have prepared for was the possibility that this eventuality would occur so soon. The suddenness of it took them by surprise, leaving them feeling shaken and guilty about the decisions they had to make.

"I feel like I'm turning her over to strangers," Emily sobbed after the move occurred. "No matter how much I tell them, they can't possibly know and do all the little things we did for her to make her more comfortable and happy."

Emily and Chad compensated for their guilt and worry by being present in Maria's new residence as much as possible.

In fact, they were there so often, they got a sobering look at how often adult children like their daughter are abandoned and neglected by their families.

"The other residents follow us down the hallway and call us 'Mom' and 'Dad' whenever we visit," Chad shared.

"You get the sense some of them haven't had visitors for years," Emily added. "It just tugs on our heart strings so to know how happy they are to see us, even when we aren't there to visit them."

Having worked with autistic children in a long-term residential facility early in my career, I could relate very well to Emily and Chad's dilemma, but I could also imagine the difficulties that staff at Maria's facility must struggle with. From the parents' perspective, nothing matters except that their child receives top-quality care, and no excuses for anything less are acceptable. From the facility's standpoint, just keeping residents safe, clean, and well-fed "twenty-four-seven" is a daunting task, especially considering that they often operate with staffs that are underpaid, under-trained and overwhelmed by their daily job stresses. For these facilities, going beyond that basic level of care with additional education and enrichment programs is often impossible; there just isn't enough time, staffing, and funding to make it all happen.

Maria's move into the long-term care center proved a bittersweet development for Emily and Chad. On the up side, Emily's heart condition began to improve once she had more rest and was doing less heavy lifting and intensive care-giving with Maria. Relations between Chad and Emily also improved greatly once the couple had more private time together. On the down side, within just a few weeks of Maria entering the program,

Emily began to notice bruises and abrasions on the girl's arms, legs, and vaginal area.

"I know she has fragile skin and bruises easily," Emily fretted in my office after this troubling new finding emerged. "But she never had any of this sort of thing happen to her when she was with us."

Emily and Chad resolved that the situation had to be reported to Protective Services, and a series of unsettling site visits and interviews ensued. At the end of the troubling process, Protective Services determined that, while no intentional abuse or neglect had occurred, facility staff needed additional training in how to minister to Maria's special dermatological needs, leaving Emily and Chad torn about whether to leave her in the center or not. In the process, they dealt with tremendous remorse about having exposed their daughter to new health risks.

"I just feel like we've abandoned her," Emily confessed. "And no matter how often I visit or how vigilant I am, I just can't get past the guilt."

I did my best to reassure both Emily and Chad that they hadn't, in fact, abandoned their daughter, and had actually done all that they could for her and more to make sure that she was as safe and healthy as possible in her new surroundings. But the reality was that they had indeed done something that violated their own wishes and values, through no fault of their own, certainly, but rather through circumstances beyond their control. Nonetheless, that didn't change the cold, hard truth that Maria was now living with strangers, outside their home, after they had spent twenty-five years doing everything in their power to keep her well.

This kind of moral or ethical dilemma is a common predicament for parents of disabled children. They know so clearly what they want for their children, and they strive so vigorously to make these ideals come true. But at the day's end, they often have to face harsh truths about their own limitations, and when they do, guilt and shame dog them mercilessly. In Emily and Chad's case, there was one more chapter in the story, the toughest chapter yet, although somehow, at its end, they would find unexpected peace and closure.

For me, the chapter opened with a voicemail from Emily saying that they needed to cancel their next therapy appointment with me, because Maria had been admitted to the hospital with a collapsed lung. By the time I got the message and returned it, I learned from Emily that Maria's other lung had also collapsed, that she was on life support and that her physicians didn't expect her to make it through the night.

"We're going to remove the life support this evening," she told me, sounding surprisingly calm. "And spend whatever time she has left with her."

The next time I would hear from Emily would be several days later when she called to inform me that Maria had passed away, but not for several days after life support had been terminated. "I told you our girl was a fighter," she said, and even over the phone, I could hear the smile in her voice. "Thing is, we didn't want her to fight anymore. She had been through so much and was in such terrible pain. We just wanted her to rest."

Maria's memorial service was one of the most moving celebrations of a human life I've ever experienced. Judging from the large, diverse crowd in attendance, there was no sense that the life we were memorializing was one that was inferior in any way. Quite the contrary, there were so many people there that I almost felt like the person we were mourning was some kind of celebrity. And, in fact, maybe Maria was.

Greeting Emily and Chad as I entered the visitation room before the service started, both hugged me warmly and told me about Maria's last hours. Turns out, they were hours spent exactly as I would have expected them to be, with mom and dad right at her side, telling her how much they loved her, singing her favorite songs, and whispering words of encouragement to their girl.

As a therapist, I've always tried over the years to make it to any special moments in clients' lives that I can when invited; baptisms, weddings, graduations, and funerals. While all of these events have been important and meaningful, each in their own way, some of them have seemed more powerful than others. Maria's service was one of those. What I sensed listening to the eulogy and watching the crowd interact at Maria's memorial, was that this was an exceptional life we were remembering; not the life of a "damaged" or "disabled" person, but an incredibly rich, full life, filled with love, laughter, friendship, and family, trips to Disney World and petting zoos, and picnics and holidays.

The next time I saw Emily and Chad for therapy would be several weeks after that beautiful service. They were still deep in their grief at the time, but also working their way toward acceptance and resolution. Emily started the session by grabbing Chad's left hand and holding it up in the air before me. There on his ring finger was the wedding band he had removed several months before when he had learned about Emily's online "affair."

"He put it back on the night Maria died," she told me, beaming.

"It just seemed the right time," Chad responded simply.

I learned that day that Emily and Chad had come a very long way in their journey to find healing, not just for the marital difficulties they had encountered, but for the grief, loss and guilt they had experienced around Maria's last months, weeks, and days. In that same session they shared an important new insight with me.

"You know, it's really ironic," Emily said. "We spent twenty-five years expecting Maria could die at any minute, and fighting our best to prevent that from happening. But we never anticipated *this* . . . what life would be like *after* she died. We hardly know what to do with ourselves some times."

Chad nodded. "It keeps feeling like we should be *doing something* right now, but there's nothing more to do."

Like most parents of adult children with disabilities, Emily and Chad had invested so much time and energy in parenting their daughter, that their very identity had come to be defined, at least to some extent, by their role as her caregivers. Now that she was gone, so too, was their prior identity, and they faced the need to re-envision their very sense of themselves and the path that the rest of their lives would take. They also still had some "loose ends" and old feelings to resolve, including their anger at the facility where Maria had lived the last months of her life.

"I'm not so noble that I haven't thought a lot about suing them," Emily admitted that day. "But in the end, what would that give us? A settlement, a check, and still no Maria. So, what's the use?"

What Emily and Chad ended up learning through these painful experiences was that they had accomplished a truly superhuman feat, by keeping a daughter who should have died in early childhood alive and well for over two decades, largely through their own love, determination, and downright stubbornness (a good thing in my book, by the way).

Chad summed it up best, I think: "We were supposed to have her for a few years. We had her for twenty-five. I figure we came out on the winning end of this one, so why should we complain?"

In the litigious world most Americans operate in these days, such grace coming to terms with tough realities is a rare commodity indeed.

Sometimes, I wonder as I'm listening to clients like Emily and Chad, just *who* is helping *who* here? So many people working in profit-driven industries spend their routine working day worrying about making the next sale, pleasing finicky customers, or impressing a demanding boss (not that there's anything wrong with that if that's what they enjoy doing). But I'm lucky enough to get to know people like Emily and Chad, who daily remind me that the human heart knows no limits.

Suggestions for Further Reading and Learning

I experienced an even greater appreciation for Emily and Chad's struggles when my literature search for articles and books on parenting adult children who are *both* mentally and physically challenged produced very few resources. Most offerings dealt with physically *or* mentally challenged children, but few dealt with children with both conditions, and even fewer with *adult* children with both conditions. One exception was *The Child Who Never Grew Up*, by award-winning author Pearl Buck, first published in 1950 and revised in 1992, which details her personal experiences raising a daughter with multiple developmental disabilities.

I found the best and most plentiful information by Googling the keywords "parenting adult children with mental and physical disabilities." There, thanks to good old Google, I found a wealth of articles, some scholarly and others personal accounts by parents. I also know from personal, professional experience that community mental health centers are mandated by federal and state standards to offer comprehensive services for mentally and physically challenged people of all ages. Parents of such children should find it helpful to contact their nearest community mental health center, although it's important to reiterate that Emily and Chad's difficulties in getting Maria's special needs met began with trained specialists' fatalistic (and inaccurate) prognosis that she would never survive beyond early childhood. As a result, parents need to be savvy consumers and advocates for their disabled children.

CHAPTER 7

Parenting vs. Grandparenting: How Needs Change When Our Kids Have Kids

Or, How to get "unstuck"

Parenting our adult children often takes on a whole new dimension once grandchildren appear on the scene. As the previous case histories have illustrated, sometimes parenting our adult children can be very challenging. Once those same adult children have their own children, family dynamics can take a turn for the better, which happened for Dora Pritchard. But sometimes family dynamics take a turn for the worse, which is what happened for Molly and Don Campbell.

Before meeting the Campbells, we need to look first at some of the special challenges grandparents *everywhere* struggle with today. In many cultures throughout history, the role of grandparent has been a revered and influential one. In most Eastern religions and in Native American spirituality, family elders have traditionally been looked up to as wisdom-keepers and mentors, to the extent that many people in these cultures actually pray to their deceased ancestors for guidance and intercession.

Similarly in African-American and Latino cultures, grandmothers, in particular, are often the functional head of the extended family, although the degree of openness with which they lead the family may vary. In many of these families, grandma may openly rule the roost as the clear, ultimate authority on every important decision. On the other hand, she may exercise a more subtle and discreet influence, deferring to the titular male head of the household, if there is one, but actually quietly and discreetly making the real decisions that keep the family afloat.

It's been my personal experience with clients in my practice that the role of grandparent has become a bit more ambiguous in white, middle-income families. Due in part to the increased mobility of many such families, where parents change jobs and families move every five to seven years, fewer grandparents live in close geographic proximity to their grandchildren today than they did two generations ago. In families where grandparents do have a close involvement with their adult children and grandchildren, their role is often something between a fairy godparent, and babysitter or back-up parent when mom and dad are away. They're expected to be helpmates, both to indulge and help watch over the kids, but also to defer largely to the kids' parents, and not "get in the way" or take on too much power. Depending on their personalities and the overall family circumstances, some grandparents may be more proactive or even intrusive rather than mere helpmates in relating to their adult children and grandchildren. But, generally speaking, the white, middle-income families I have known have assigned a more secondary role to grandparents, and parents have often rebelled at grandparents trying to exercise too much authority over the grandkids.

Across cultures in America today, there are countless families where parents can't manage to care for their children on their own, and have to rely on *their* parents for help. A recent AARP study found that 6.3 percent of all children in the United States under the age of eighteen are living full-time with grandparents, and that households headed by a grandparent had increased by 30 percent since 1990. It's in these families where family relationships, roles, and boundaries often become extremely confused and conflicted; and that's exactly what first brought the Campbells into therapy with me.

Molly and Don Campbell were a hard-working, blue-collar couple. He worked on an assembly line at the local Ford truck plant; she was a teacher's aide at a local elementary school. They made a fairly comfortable living by pooling their two modest incomes and living frugally for the most part. However, they found that once their first granddaughter Annie arrived, they had a difficult time restraining themselves from spending money on gifts for the baby. Some of these were necessities that their only child, twenty-two-year-old son Mark, and his wife Susie, had a hard time providing on Mark's erratic income as a journeyman electrician; disposable diapers, formula, infant clothes, and such. But, some of these were also niceties that Molly and Don wanted their grandchild to have; toys, furniture, and educational aides that Mark and Susie could never have provided.

Early on, the Campbells set a precedent of stepping in to help their son and his family financially. At first, Mark and Susie seemed genuinely appreciative, but before long, Molly and Don became concerned that the kids not only depended on their help, but also came to expect it and take it for granted.

"I'm glad to lend a hand anytime I can," Molly told me in our first session. "But I've already raised my own family. I can't raise theirs, too. Especially not when they don't even thank me anymore for the things we provide. Susie actually called me the other day with a list of things she needed for the baby, and hung up after she was done, without so much as a 'please' or 'thank you.' It was like she just knew I'd come through with the goods, so she didn't even have to pretend to be polite."

To their credit, the Campbells had already recognized and acknowledged their role in creating the dilemma they were experiencing. "What's the old saying," Don asked with a rueful smile in that first meeting. "Something about how 'no good deed goes unpunished?'"

An old axiom in the mental health field tells us "insight produces behavior change," but sometimes just knowing something needs to be done doesn't make the road to accomplishing it any easier. The Campbells knew even before they came to see me that they needed to do things differently with their son and his family, but they didn't know how to begin. Things took a downward spiral when Mark took a steady but low-paying job out of town; Susie and the baby were going to have to give up their small apartment and find new housing. To complicate matters further, Susie announced that she was pregnant again.

"I can go live with my Mom," Susie told Molly and Don, but the very idea struck fear in their hearts. Susie's mom was a known drug addict, who lived in subsidized housing in a rough part of town where violent crime was a constant problem. The thought of their grandbaby and daughter-in-law living there was out of the question for them.

So, in another good deed they would ultimately come to regret, the Campbells invited Susie and the baby to come live in their finished basement. In one of his last family moments before heading off to his new job, Mark moved them all into the basement with Don and Molly's help. Susie came down with a migraine that day and provided no assistance whatsoever.

"Except to get in the way," Molly fumed in my office the following week. "And complain that she needed Mark to do this or that for her!" The Campbells' multi-generational family experience was off to a very shaky start indeed. Unfortunately, it would get even shakier before it got better.

Once Mark was gone, Susie fell into a deep depression aggravated by the terrible morning sickness and loneliness she was experiencing. Some days she couldn't (or *wouldn't*, Molly opined) get out of bed to care for the baby. Molly and Don had to take off sick days from work just to make sure the baby was fed and changed. Within a few short, tumultuous weeks, the Campbells had lost complete control of their home, their work, and their personal lives, all thanks to their own generosity and compassion.

"But, what else could we do?" Don queried in therapy with me shortly afterward. "Susie's a high school dropout who's never had a job except waiting tables. If she went to live with her mom, it would be just a matter of time before we'd be calling Child Protective Services to save our granddaughter from God knows what."

Sadly, he was right, and I was able to genuinely support him and Molly for the decision they had made. "Some decisions are no-brainers," I reassured them. "No matter how difficult the consequences, we just have to do the right thing. Having Susie and the baby join you was the right thing, even if the consequences mean dealing with lots of 'wrong things.' Now, our job is to figure out how to make the best of the situation you find yourself in."

But even as I was trying to comfort the Campbells, I wondered how they could make the best of their situation. As a therapist with almost four decades of experience under my belt, I sometimes feel like I've seen and done a bit of everything. As a result, it's rare that I find myself "stumped" anymore. Still, I was thoroughly stumped on this one.

Comparing notes with colleagues or attending professional conferences over the years, I've often found myself engaged in conversations about how to deal with clients' "stuck-ness." Therapists refer to a client being "stuck" when both the client and the therapist are saying all the right words and doing all the right things, but no progress toward stated goals is occurring. Obviously, this can be a frustrating and even damaging place for clients and therapists to be, as the shared sense of immobilization can sabotage the therapy process. Often clients drop out of care, or therapists suggest a sabbatical from treatment at these times. The latter strikes me as a true "cop out" by the way, but each of us has to handle our professional obstacles in our own way, I suppose.

A Jungian conceptual framework provides the most helpful ideas I've encountered for dealing with client stuck-ness. Jung believed in the importance of what he called "holding the tension," which occurs when the psyche is dealing with being "*between* one thing and another," whether it be a relationship, a life stage, a job change, or whatever. There, in that place *in between things*, he believed, the psyche, (the Greek word for *soul*), does some of its most important work.

Under this definition of stuck-ness, rather than chafing at being stuck with our clients, we would reframe the situation as an opportunity to learn something, and would explore several key reflective questions together:

- Everything that happens can have meaning. What might be the meaning behind the present dilemma?
- What is the psyche asking of us now?
- What are we being called upon to learn or change?
- Once we think we know the answers to these questions, how do we make it happen?
- Do we need to do something positive and proactive? If so, what steps and what other people might that involve?
- Or, on the contrary, do we need to introspect and ponder things in our hearts? If so, what are some ways we can do that (meditation, prayer, gardening, jogging, etc.)?

The Campbells certainly had a lot to "ponder in their hearts." They had just seen their only child off to a faraway, long-term job. They had surrendered the serenity they felt in their comfortable home to a whining, passive-dependent daughter-in-law. And they were now at risk of losing the good performance records they had at work over their frequent absences due to caring for grandbaby Annie.

When I began to pose these questions to them, I wasn't prepared for how well they would embrace the introspection process, and how rich their responses would be. As we began to explore some of the possible reasons behind their present impasse, they threw uncomfortable glances at each other and exchanged embarrassed smiles.

"Guess I need to get something else out on the table now," Don admitted. "I quit drinking a couple of months ago after putting away a twelve-pack every day since I was a teenager . . . sometimes it was a whole case of beer over a weekend. It's been pretty uncomfortable going without it sometimes."

"He has trouble keeping his mind off it," Molly chimed in. "He does better when he's busy doing something all the time."

"Like taking care of others?" I asked, and he nodded.

"So when life is placid you struggle with cravings," I suggested. "But when things get a little crazy and chaotic you're better off . . . you can focus on others instead of yourself?"

"*Exactly*," he said, looking relieved to have this important puzzle piece out on the table. "But I need to admit something else. I kinda feel superior, because I'm so good with the baby and Susie's not. She's a lousy mother, really. But, I can't tell her that, or tell her how to parent her own kid. It's just easier to do it myself . . . though I guess that doesn't help Susie learn how to do things any better, does it?"

"That's a really important insight," I said.

Molly jumped in again. "It's not all his stuff," she confessed. "After Mark was born, I wanted more kids . . . Don didn't." She seemed surprised to find herself welling up with tears, but struggled to keep talking. "In spite of all the problems, I think I feel more like a real 'mom' with Susie and the baby in our home. I'd really like to find a way to make it work, but I'm not sure my motives are so pure. To be honest, I'd think I'd really like to have the babies for my own and get Susie out of their lives."

Numerous authors in the field of communications have addressed the role hidden agendas play in obstructing effective communication and problem-solving. The Campbells had just demonstrated a textbook example. Both had been coming to therapy regularly and working hard in it, yet we had all reached an impasse together somehow. How could any of us have known that two powerful pieces of history, the troubled feelings Molly and Don harbored about seemingly irrelevant issues, his alcohol abuse and her unmet mothering needs, could have been at the heart of the impasse? But, by keeping these feelings secret, the Campbells had given the feelings power over them, causing them to withhold information and miss important opportunities to clear the air and salve their consciences. Their secret-keeping had also prevented them from getting some simple reassurance from their therapist that these feelings were perfectly normal and understandable, causing them needless worry and guilt that clouded their judgment and impeded their progress.

Clearly these issues and history were laden with powerful emotions for both Molly and Don. When I posed the question, "What was the psyche asking of them?" they went right to the core.

"To grow up and learn to live without my beer or any other kind of crutch, including taking care of others," Don sighed.

Molly welled up with tears again. "To get over my grief and close the book on the past," she whispered.

Now that we had identified and dispelled all hidden agendas, with the whole truth out at last, the Campbells' work began to move forward in truly substantive ways. They readily acknowledged the need to be more firm with Susie about getting professional help for her depression, so that she could take better care of her own child, and free them from the grandparenting responsibilities that were causing them conflict at work. Another step forward, was that Don recognized the need to get some outside help for his alcohol issues, rather than "self-medicating" them by caring for others. Both Molly and Don admitted that they might benefit from some sort of support groups, in addition to their couple counseling with me, an alcoholism recovery group for Don, and for Molly a codependency group (there's *that word* again).

In the weeks and sessions to come, the Campbells reported considerable progress on their goals. First, they managed to get Susie to agree to see a therapist, and consider starting anti-depressant medications, once they could get the advice of a psychiatrist as to what was safe for pregnant women to take. Susie did begin therapy and was surprised to find that she really enjoyed it. Getting an appointment with a psychiatrist was in the works, although they were frustrated that many of the doctors they called didn't accept Susie's state-issued medical card, and didn't have appointments available for several months. Both Molly and Don began attending support groups, and like Susie, were surprised to find how much they enjoyed them.

In yet another surprise, Mark came home from his out-of-town job long before his assignment there was over. He had injured his back in a fall from high scaffolding and was lucky to be alive, but he was temporarily disabled. There was a frightening prospect of his becoming permanently disabled if a recommended delicate and dangerous back surgery didn't succeed. Despite being pleased to have Mark alive and safe at home, the prospect of having another marginalized adult child in their home, unable to pull his own weight, worried Molly and Don greatly, and rightfully so.

In response to this development, and in the biggest surprise of all, Susie rallied and found herself a job as a receptionist at a local hair salon. It didn't pay much, but it sure beat having no income at all, and she seemed excited and proud to be contributing something to the family finances, especially at a time when Mark was unable to work.

Molly and Don ended their work with me several months after Mark came home, when their second grandchild arrived, a little boy named Dylan.

"It's crazier than ever in that house now," Don laughed in our last session. "But, that's not why we're quitting for now. It's because we're actually pretty happy with the way things are here lately."

Molly chimed in. "Oh, we'll probably be back some day," she said. "Probably with the kids and grandkids in tow. But the kids are paying us a little rent now, buying more of their own food and other things . . . but here's the best part; they seem to really enjoy being together without us down in their own space and taking care of the kids themselves. We actually hear them laughing and playing all the time."

"And that's a wonderful sound," Don smiled.

So as all grandparents must do, Molly and Don had found the balance it takes to continue parenting their adult children effectively once grandchildren arrive. They had learned how be supportive and helpful without taking over and enabling their children, thereby keeping the kids from learning important parenting and life skills such as making a living, paying bills, and feeding and clothing their children.

But first, the Campbells had needed to get good and *stuck*, wallowing as long as they needed to in their own individual, marital and family dilemmas until things became uncomfortable enough to motivate them to change. Similarly, as their therapist, I had needed to wallow in the bog along with them a while, in order to figure out what they needed from me to move forward.

SUGGESTIONS FOR FURTHER READING AND LEARNING

Readers wanting to know more about effectively parenting adult children, while also grandparenting will find the following readings and resources helpful.

Jay, J. and Cline, F.W. *Grandparenting with Love and Logic: Practical Solutions to Today's Grandparenting Challenges.* Golden, CO: The Love & Logic Press, 1994. (Also visit the Love and Logic Institute website at www.loveandlogic.com)

Kemp, G., Kovatch, S., and Goldstein, A. (2010). "Grandparenting Tips: Building Great Relationships with Your Grandkids." Online article available at www.helpguide.org/mental/grandparenting.htm.

Kornhaber, A. *The Grandparent Guide: The Definitive Guide to Coping with the Challenges of Modern Grandparenting.* New York, NY: Contemporary Books, 2010.

CHAPTER 8

Step-Parenting Issues in Blended Families

Or, "There's a reason so many fairy tales have wicked stepmothers!"

In his 1974 best-seller, *Scripts People Live*, Claude Steiner asserted that most people are born "Okay" but that sometime in childhood, many of us develop life "scripts" that then become our navigational charts for the rest of our lives. Scripts emerge from all sorts of relationships and influences in our lives, but especially from parents. The fairy tales, myths, and role models that we embrace as children also have a role in determining our life scripts.

Steiner likened the nurturing parent to a good witch or guardian angel who affirms and supports the child, sending them out into the world under a positive "spell," whereby good things come to them. Conversely, he likened the critical parent to a bad witch who puts a curse on the child, bringing them a lifetime of hardship and struggle. As we saw in earlier chapters dealing with roles in dysfunctional families, scripts may serve some function in our lives, but are ultimately self-limiting and even downright pathogenic, resulting in true mental illness, addiction, and broken lives. Scripts can also function at a larger socio-cultural level. This happens when we come to believe something as a society or a nation that results in negative expectations for certain demographic groups, such as "illegal aliens," creating an oppressive social order for them.

The relevance of all this for our discussion about parenting adult children is that it shines light on a dynamic that exists in many blended families. Stepparents often struggle to overcome negative societal scripts about stepparenting, which may have been internalized by their stepchildren. This is evidenced by a common remark from these children: "You're not my *real* parent. I don't have to listen to you."

There's a long history of negative perceptions about stepparents. Consider the number of fairy tales that include evil stepparent characters, usually wicked stepmothers, but occasionally wicked stepfathers as well. The presence of the malevolent stepparent archetype in world literature across time and diverse cultures speaks to a basic, global assumption that only a true *biological* parent can be a "real" parent; also that any stepparent can't possibly have the best interests of the child at heart, and in fact, is probably ultimately dangerous to the child.

Intellectually, we all know better, of course. Using our rational minds and powers of observation, we can look around and see many blended families where stepparents and stepchildren love each other deeply and live together happily. The problem is, using those same rational processes most of us can also see blended families where they *don't*.

Therein lies the heart of the matter: stepparenting is a special, challenging role, fraught with unique stresses and pitfalls that not everyone handles well. The stepparent who manages it gracefully is usually an especially child-centered individual who is loving and loyal, and isn't daunted by hard work or being tested. And just as being a biological parent can get more complicated once children become adults, so can stepparenting.

Being a loving and effective stepparent requires many of the same skills we've already talked about in earlier chapters:

- Focusing on strengths in solving problems
- Setting clear boundaries
- Using whole messages
- Reeling in projections
- Practicing assertiveness skills, and
- Utilizing creative conflict resolution strategies.

But, it also calls on both biological parents and stepparents to master another skill set described as "principled negotiation techniques," best summarized in David and Frank Johnson's book *Joining Together: Group Theory and Group Skills*. These include:

- *Jointly* agreeing on a definition of the conflict
- Exchanging *feelings* about the conflict and *proposals* for solutions
- Recognizing the conflict as a *mutual problem to be solved*, not as a win-lose struggle
- *Reversing perspectives* or trying to walk in each other's shoes to understand the other's viewpoint
- Imagining options for *mutual* benefit
- Reaching a *reasoned and reasonable agreement*, and
- Repeating all of the above steps, over and over, until *complete success* finally results.

As both a therapist and a management consultant working with several large, troubled agencies and organizations over the years, I've utilized Johnson and Johnson's principled negotiation guidelines countless times and have always found them to be extremely effective with both micro problems (small, interpersonal situations), as well as macro situations (large-scale, systemic problems).

In my practice with blended families, I've been fortunate to know mainly "good witch" stepparents, although I've certainly heard plenty about the "wicked" ones, too. I have also known my fair share of stepparents who were neither "good" nor "wicked" particularly, but who struggled mightily with the role and made plenty of mistakes, often with the best of intentions.

Dottie Thomas's husband, Jake, was a perfect example of the latter type. An attractive couple in their late forties, Dottie and Jake owned and operated a popular health spa, which demanded a great deal of their time. Dottie had been married before to an abusive alcoholic, whom she divorced when her two children, Billy and Jill, were just toddlers. After struggling for a while on her own, living in her parents' basement, she met Jake at a church social. The two fell in love and eloped after a whirlwind courtship.

Despite their mutual attraction, what Dottie hadn't considered before getting married to Jake was just what kind of a father he might make. He had always been totally charming to her kids the few times he saw them before the wedding, bringing them gifts and making a big fuss over them. Unfortunately, once they were married, only then did it become clear to Dottie that Jake just didn't have a nurturing bone in his body.

"Oh, it's not like he was abusive in any way," she told me.

"He just didn't 'get' kids. They would ask for something simple they needed and instead of just saying, 'Okay, here it is,' he would sit and question with them whether they really needed it after all. I'd see the look on the kids' faces and I could tell they were thinking, 'What's wrong with this guy,' but they never disrespected him. Over time, they all found a way to work together. Jill learned how to wrap Jake around her little finger, then do whatever she wanted when he was looking the other way. Billy just gave him a wide berth, and tried to not need much of anything at all from him. And we all got through the years pretty well, I'd say."

Things got more difficult once the kids were grown, and began experiencing more adult issues and challenges in their own lives. Just as he hadn't been able to understand or empathize with their needs as small children, Jake couldn't relate to them any better as adults. In fact, he seemed to relate to them even worse, especially Billy. In a classic alpha male struggle, Jake began to vie for dominance with Billy when the young man came home to live with them after flunking out of college at age twenty two. Dottie could see that her son was deeply depressed and needed a safe place to heal. But Jake wanted Billy to "earn his keep" and was constantly after him about one thing or another.

"In Jake's eyes, Billy basically couldn't do anything right," Dottie told me, remembering those days. "I'd see the struggle going on inside my son as he tried to stand up to his stepdad but the boy was just so depleted inside at the time that it was never a fair fight. Jake really did a number on Billy's mental health, and I blame myself for not stepping up to the plate and doing a better job of protecting my son."

Dottie had just revealed a common dilemma experienced by

many blended family parents. Knowing their own child inside out, the biological parent often sees what their child needs when the stepparent doesn't, but in the interest of keeping peace or "not taking sides," they defer to the stepparent, leaving the child feeling abandoned and betrayed.

Things finally came to a head when Jake and Billy got into a physical altercation with each other. Jake had walked into Billy's room uninvited when the young man was having a particularly bad day, and ordered him to, "Clean up this pig sty and get a life!" Billy snapped, and the two men ended up in a wrestling match that Dottie had a hard time interrupting.

"I really thought they were going to kill each other," she told me. "I actually think if I hadn't been there, that they might have."

After that, there was clearly no way the two contentious men could live under the same roof together. Billy made plans to move in with a friend who needed a roommate, and within days he was gone from Dottie and Jake's house. "And from my life, too, for a while," Dottie added sadly. "I guess he felt like I'd made my choice and it was Jake, not him. I don't know if I'll ever be able to forgive myself for that."

When she did finally reconnect with him a few weeks later, Billy was actually doing better than Dottie had seen him be for a long while. He had gotten a job, enrolled in school, and liked his new roommate and apartment.

"I think he felt good about himself, striking out on his own and paying his own way. Young men need to feel like they can take care of themselves."

Dottie and her family had come through a major firestorm relatively intact after all, it seemed. But, there were still lots of unresolved issues on the table and she was determined to have a better life for herself and her kids, and a better marriage with Jake. That involved bringing him into our sessions, which would be the place where things really began to become clearer for Dottie.

In the weeks following Billy's move, I saw Dottie with Jake a number of times for marital counseling. In these sessions, I was able to hear directly from him in his own words why he had parented Billy the way he did. As a result, I came to see that Jake wasn't a bad man. He certainly didn't deserve the title of "wicked stepfather." He had just committed one of the biggest mistakes any parent can ever make, and that's assuming he was right and everyone else was wrong. This mistake is perhaps even more disastrous for stepparents when they override the child's biological parent with their "greater wisdom" about what's best for the child.

Dottie thoroughly understood Billy's emotional temperament and needs. But Jake had an agenda for Billy, always a problem in interpersonal communication, as we've seen in previous chapters. He was going "to teach Billy to be a man" the hard way, by forcing his will on the young man and *making* him do what Jake considered to be the right things: getting a job, cleaning his room, and rousing himself from bed, even when he was massively depressed. There might have even been a degree of wisdom in his ideas, but not in the way he imposed them on Billy and on Dottie, as well.

Marital therapy for Dottie and Jake proved to be a matter of "too little, too late." After several sessions, Dottie realized that Jake wasn't open to changing his ways or even considering viewpoints other than his own. So much damage had occurred to their marriage over the years that his recent treatment of Billy became the catalyst for her to make a long overdue decision, telling Jake she wanted a divorce.

What Dottie and Jake's experience clarifies for us is the importance of principled negotiation between parents and stepparents in blended family situations. Neither one of them was all right or all wrong. They each had worthwhile ideas about how to improve their family life, but Jake made it impossible for any kind of discussion or negotiation to occur by asserting his male dominance and trying to play, "Father Knows Best."

If we had all come together sooner, and had more time before the crises ensued to do some preventive work, Dottie and Jake could have benefited greatly from some coaching in principled negotiation techniques. They could have defined their family's problems as opportunities to all learn something and grow closer together, rather than a mere power struggle where someone had to be right, or *win*, and someone had to be wrong, or *lose*.

Nonetheless, whatever missed opportunities we might have had, I was pleased to see both Dottie and Billy overcome the damage the last few years had wrought on all of them. I've continued to see Dottie, and Billy too, for individual therapy on and off since her divorce, and have been pleased to watch both of them recover completely from their emotional wounds. Coincidentally, she's now engaged to a man with two teenaged children and she is becoming a stepmother to them. Having seen her interact with her new stepchildren at my office a number of times, I feel confident she's going to be the "fairy godmother" kind of stepmother.

If Dottie and Jake Thomas were a classic "what-might-have-been" story, Ann and Bill Axton were a classic example of getting it right the first time. While they first came to me for marital counseling, it soon became clear that the Axtons' marital problems were all due to conflicts they were having stepparenting their four adult children. Each of them had two children from previous marriages, a son and a daughter apiece, and each was also close to their own biological kids, but had major tensions with their stepchildren. The gist of these various tensions was that the kids tended to engage in triangulation, a problematic dynamic addressed in an earlier chapter. The kids would be polite and agreeable to their stepparents in the presence of their biological parent, but talked down or even told outright lies about the stepparent later when the stepparent wasn't around.

Things had reached a critical mass recently when Ann and Bill had drawn up wills, and the kids took issue with the terms in them. Kentucky is a community property state, where it's the norm for spouses to leave their entire estate to each other. Kids on both sides expressed their fears that their stepparent wouldn't will them any of the estate that remained at their own death.

"She's never liked me, and I know she's going to cut me off without a penny," Bill's kids complained to him when Ann wasn't there.

"He's always had it in for me, and I know he'll just love sticking it to me when you're gone," Ann's children predicted.

Unfortunately, the constant harangue from their kids had eventually cut into Ann and Bill's trust for each other.

"I don't know that I can really trust him to do the right thing by my kids if I do go first," Ann confessed in our first session.

Bill responded in kind. "Now admit it, Ann. You really don't like my kids and they have good reason to doubt your intentions."

As a career psychotherapist, I've often found it curious that couples can argue quite heatedly about something that *hasn't even happened yet*, but rather just *might* occur somewhere down the road. What these situations generally reveal is the important *unconscious* power certain issues in their lives hold over them. Ann and Bill were both physically fit, middle-aged people who promised to have a long and healthy life ahead of them. But here they were, arguing like barristers about what the other might do to harm their children. Clearly, there was some other puzzle piece we hadn't stumbled upon yet.

Numerous texts on counseling techniques talk about the importance of asking clients the question, "Why is this matter surfacing here and why is it important now?" When I asked Ann and Bill this question, they both seemed totally befuddled.

"Quite frankly, I'm not sure," Ann admitted, with a perplexed smile.

"Ditto," Bill said and threw his wife a sheepish grin. "Do you think we may have just 'been had,' huh?" Ann nodded yes.

Unknowingly, the Axtons had just stumbled upon and completed the first step in a principled negotiation process. Through their recognition that the matter at hand wasn't a pressing or immediate one, and that their children had managed to amplify and dramatize it in an effort to drive a wedge between the two of them, they were able redefine the problem as a parent-child communication issue, rather than a marital relations one. Having done that, they were then able to vent their frustration with the kids, and come to see the conflict as a problem they shared with their kids, rather than a win-lose struggle between the two of them.

They had a little more trouble with the task of walking in each others' shoes to understand the other person's viewpoint.

Ann had previously been married to a terribly abusive man, and she and her kids had learned to cleave very close to each other to survive, causing her to become an extremely vigilant and protective mother. When they needed her for anything at all, Ann's initial and most powerful response was to be there totally for them and ask questions later. She was one of those "I'd-do-anything-for-my-kids" parents. On the other hand, Bill had experienced a relatively amicable divorce from a woman he still liked and respected, largely because the two just grew apart over the years due to their demanding careers. His kids had seen the divorce coming and accepted it fairly well for the most part, so he had no strong need to protect them from life's stresses, and had a hard time understanding Ann's needs to do so with her kids.

Sometimes in couples counseling, we just need to ask partners to acknowledge to each other, "I don't get where you're coming from here, but I support you nonetheless." That was the magic key Ann needed from Bill; knowing that even though he didn't completely understand her thinking and feeling in this instance, he still "had her back." Once he was able to express that reassurance to her, they were able to begin imagining options for mutual gain, and reaching a reasoned and reasonable agreement. What they eventually worked out had a justice and symmetry to it that I had to smile about when they shared it with me.

"We called everyone together for a 'summit meeting'," Bill began the story and Ann picked it up from there.

"We sat them all down together and asked them, 'Are you in a hurry for us to die? Because if you are, we can just go on and give you your inheritance now so you won't have to worry about getting what you're due and letting it come between us all.'"

At this point, they told me, the sons had begun to sputter and protest how silly this all was, while the daughters had put their hands to their faces and cried embarrassed tears.

Bill summed the story up. "We ended by telling them that if any of them ever wanted to talk to us about our spouse, we'd call the spouse and have them sit in with us while they did. That was two weeks ago, and everyone has been so *damned* happy and agreeable ever since then . . . I wish we'd done this *years* ago!"

Another core principle of family systems theory is that in order for a family to be happy and "functional," the strongest relationship in it has to be the marital bond between parents. Whenever a child can intrude in that bond and distance the parents from each other, the whole family, and especially the marriage, is at risk. That principle holds true *especially* with stepparents in blended family situations, where alliances and divisions are already complex, and family history on both sides is often *complicated* and *complicating.*

Some cold, hard truths can help parents rally motivation to protect their marriage on this score.

Truth One: Our children are some of our greatest joys and comforts in life; but few of us have contracts and agreements with them about how they plan to care for us in our old age. They may support and nurture us or they may not. So, it's folly to predicate any decisions about how to interact with them now on concerns about their future caretaking role with us, especially when the tie between them and us is a stepparent/stepchild relationship.

Truth Two: The role of the child in most parent-child relationships is essentially a narcissistic one. This isn't because our children are selfish or egocentric by the way; it's just part of our hard-wiring as mammals and primates, a species in which the parent-child and especially the mother-child bond is particularly life-giving and thus powerful. No matter how much our children love us, and no matter how adult and independent they become, they will always be our children and the core power differential in that parent-child relationship is very difficult, if not impossible, to transcend. They will generally be much more concerned about how *we* are meeting *their* needs, than they are with how *they* are meeting *our* needs. Once again, this power differential is even more complex and difficult to manage in stepparent/stepchild relationships.

Truth Three: Conversely, in a perfect world, our children are *supposed* to leave us. We can know that our job as parents is done when our kids no longer *depend* on us for their survival. But, despite knowing this innately, for most parents the actual *letting go* of their children is often a difficult process. Many of us place all kinds of "hooks" under our kids' skins, even as we purport to be setting them free. These hooks bring them home to roost with and depend on us again, largely to meet our own emotional "needs to be needed." These issues may be amplified in blended family situations where biological roots versus marital/societal roots often come into question; i.e. "I can barely figure out my relationship with my own son, and now my stepson is jerking my chain! That and now my spouse is telling me I'm being insensitive to her child!"

Given all this, it's easy to see why blended families, and stepparents and stepchildren struggle so hard to make sense of their lives and relationships. Fortunately, the Axtons had come to the realization that their children, despite loving them deeply, were more concerned about their own welfare than they were about their parents' happiness. Having faced that sad reality, they were then able to redirect their kids' behavior, and regain control of some damaging family dynamics that were heading them all toward an ultimate train wreck.

Suggestions for Further Reading and Learning

Readers wanting to know more about effective conflict resolution strategies and principled negotiation techniques will find the followings readings helpful:

Johnson, D. and Johnson, F. *Joining Together: Group Theory and Group Skills*. Needham Heights, MA: Allyn and Bacon, 1994.

McKay, M., Davis, M., and Fanning, P. *Messages: The Communication Skills Book*. Oakland, CA: New Harbinger Publications, 1995.

McKay, M., Davis, M., and Fanning, P. *Thoughts & Feelings: Taking Control of Your Moods and Your Life*. Oakland, CA: New Harbinger Publications, 2007.

CHAPTER 9

Grieving and Healing When an Adult Child Dies

Or, "It isn't fair . . . I was supposed to go first."

We've already looked several times at how devastating the loss of a child is for a parent, no matter what the age of the child might be. In earlier chapters, we saw how Christy Duncan, Emily Hernandez and Chad Curtis grieved the loss of their adult children, and began the healing process for their mourning. However, each of their situations was somewhat unique; Christy's daughter Kelly hadn't died, but had intentionally cut her family out of her life; and Emily and Chad's daughter Maria had been a developmentally disabled child who they always knew could die at any time due to her high-risk health problems. As a result, perhaps their case histories are not the usual experience most parents go through when an adult child dies, if there is such a thing as a "usual experience" in this matter.

That said, over the years I've worked with several parents mourning the loss of an adult child who all shared certain common feelings and experiences. They all went through the same stages of grief that Kubler-Ross identified decades ago in her landmark book *On Death and Dying*: denial, bargaining, anger, depression, and ultimately acceptance. They all experienced these stages in their own personal way, not necessarily in any chronological, linear fashion, but as a flood of many stages often overlapping each other as time went by. They all eventually found greater peace and eventual healing through the presence of some sort of spirituality in their lives, a topic we'll explore both in this chapter and in a later chapter more deeply.

Some other norms have emerged in my work with these parents. For starters, it has seemed to me that parents of an adult child who had been ill for a long time worked through their grief sooner and more peacefully, probably because the family was prepared to some extent for their imminent loss. That's not to say these parents' loss was any less painful or difficult; just that it had been expected and thus they had been able to engage in some anticipatory grieving before the child's death.

It has also seemed true to me that parents of adult children who have died in a sudden accident or other traumatic event, such as a murder or suicide, grieved in a way that was more dramatic and intense, dwelling longer in the anger stage and taking longer to reach acceptance. Parents' grieving can be even more complicated if the child's death came about due to substance abuse, such as drunk driving or a drug overdose. Mattie Bennett was such a parent.

A proud African-American woman with a regal bearing, Mattie was the widowed matriarch of a large family that included four sons and four daughters. She had struggled to raise her children on a widow's pension after her husband, a railroad lineman, had been killed when he slipped and fell under a moving train.

Through hard work and thrift, she had managed to get them all through school, and even see most of them win scholarships and graduate from college, then go into the professions of nursing, teaching, and social work. Unfortunately, that wasn't the case for her youngest, her twenty-five-year-old son Avery.

"He was always in some kind of trouble," she recalled in our first session. "It just seemed to follow him around like a dark cloud over his head." I soon learned that Avery had been her most intelligent child, but that he had also been acutely aware of his gifts, and had learned early on that he didn't really have to work too hard to get good grades in school and make life go his way; that is, until he became a teenager and got involved in the drug abuse and gang life that permeated the family's tough West Louisville neighborhood.

"He went in and out of rehab and juvenile corrections centers for years," Mattie told me. "But when he turned eighteen, they threw him into the adult corrections system. And that was the worst thing in the world for him."

Now an adult offender, Avery lost no time hooking up with the most violent and dangerous offenders he met while incarcerated for numerous offenses, from vandalism to drug dealing. "It was like he thought they were actually something *special*," Mattie reminisced. "The more tattoos they had and the longer their rap sheets, the more he wanted to get to know them, even take after them like a moth to a flame."

Mattie had sought her own personal counseling and parenting guidance several times over the years, and was well-versed in tough love principles. When Avery turned twenty-one, the family did an intervention with him, and offered him the choice of either entering a long-term treatment program, or leaving

Mattie's house and making it on his own on the streets. Not surprisingly, Avery chose the streets. That was beginning of years of worry and stress for Mattie, as she watched her youngest son descend into a life of worsening crime, eventually landing in complete and total dereliction.

"The last time I saw him, he came by the house to ask me for some money," she said, tears filling her eyes. "He was thin as a rail and sickly looking. But he said he was going to get clean and sober, go out and find a real job. He said he was done with the streets . . . some bad people were after him and he wanted a better life for himself. And do you know what I did? I *laughed!* My baby asked me for my help and I *laughed* at him!"

Avery left Mattie's house that night with empty pockets and an angry slam of the door behind him. She knew better than to enable his habit by lending him money, and had come to expect the worst from him any time he had money to buy drugs. But what she didn't expect was that she would never see him alive again. Later that same night, Mattie awoke to the sound of banging on her door. When she went to the door, she found two police officers standing there and they didn't have to say a word.

"I just looked in their eyes and I knew," she said, tears trickling down her cheeks. "They said there had been a big wreck down on River Road . . . several cars and a motorcycle all piled up together. Avery was a passenger in one of the cars . . . I didn't recognize the driver's name but I can only assume it was one of his junkie friends. The coroner's report said they were all high on a bunch of different drugs and alcohol . . ." She trailed off into a wordless grief, turning the damp handkerchief in her hand over and over again.

As I listened to Mattie's story, and watched the pain she emanated, I thought I'd never seen a more bereft and guilt-ridden parent. Given all that, the question looming for both of us now was how to help her find healing for such a deep, almost bottomless well of sadness.

Always a survivor, who had overcome countless obstacles and hardships over the years, Mattie had wandered into new territory for her . . . a land of doubt and fear and hopelessness. Following Avery's death, she lapsed into a major depression, sleeping sixteen hours a day, and never changing out of her nightgown, getting up only to eat a bowl of cereal and watch some television in her recliner, where she would usually just fall asleep again. Her other children would call or drop by her house, wanting to take her out to lunch or to go shopping, but she always declined. "I just don't have the energy today," she would tell them.

Finally her oldest daughter, Denise, did a one-woman intervention of her own with Mattie. Barging her way into her mom's house, Denise stood with her hands on her hips and declared, "It's over, Mama! This has got to end. You go in there and get dressed and we're going to go out and find you help."

Mattie chuckled as she told me the story. "She always was strong-headed, that girl. But she was right, and I'm thankful she did me that way."

Denise had driven Mattie to the home of their minister, where the three had had coffee and talked about what to do. Despite her depression, Mattie's faith had never wavered; she just hadn't had the energy to get up and go to church.

"Reverend Steven told me he needed plenty of help and I was just the person to fill the job." Mattie recounted how she had signed up that day to deliver meals to the housebound several days a week, and help out in the church's day care center several other days of the week. Before long, she was deeply immersed in caring for numerous people who had burdens equal to or worse than her own, and found herself ruminating less about her own loss, and worrying more about how to help others with theirs.

Despite her progress through these activities, Mattie still struggled with depression and horrific mental images of Avery's last moments of life. It was as a result of these symptoms that her family had finally encouraged her to seek professional counseling. Her health insurance carrier had channeled her to me, because I was listed in their directory as a specialist in grief and loss issues.

When we first met, Mattie was clearly already on her way to healing. So what else did we need to do to help her even further on that path? The answers soon emerged from the focus of her dialogues with me. In her very first session, she must have referred to her son's *face* at least a dozen times. "He had such a sweet, funny *face* . . . his *face* just fell when I told him I wasn't giving him any more money . . . if I could only see my baby's *face* for real just one more time . . ."

Taking that cue, I asked her if she had any pictures of Avery, and she promptly produced a wallet accordion pack of photos. Looking at them with her, I was struck by how handsome he was, looking much like a young Marvin Gaye, before the drugs and alcohol got to him, too. When I told her so, she sighed.

"Not the last few months," she said. "The crystal meth took all the flesh out of his cheeks and his teeth were going bad."

I just nodded, having seen many times over the years the terrible toll this poisonous drug takes on its users. I learned from Mattie that she had been so depressed after Avery's death that she had elected to have a small private church service and burial conducted by Reverend Steven; she just hadn't been up to the usual viewings, full funeral service, and wake. When I asked her if she planned to have some sort of a memorial eventually, I was surprised by the vehemence of her response. She drew back in her chair and glared at me. "I'm not ready to just file him away like that!"

So, there we were in a true conundrum. Mattie was coming to see me for grief counseling, having suffered with a painful bereavement for several months now. But, she still wasn't fully past the initial denial that her son was dead. I could understand her need to hold out on a final ceremony, and I supported her in that decision for the time being. Everyone needs to grieve on their own timeline, I knew. As a result, we shifted gears and focused on other issues and techniques for the next few sessions. Once again, following her lead in talking about Avery's face, it occurred to me that Mattie might benefit from some Gestalt "empty chair" work.

Though we hear less about it in recent years, the time was when Gestalt therapy was all the rage and lots of therapists used the empty chair technique. The process uses elements of both creative visualization and psychodrama, as clients sit before an empty chair and imagine someone sitting there with whom they have unresolved feelings or issues. The therapist guides the client in having a dialogue with the person in the other chair in an effort to vicariously work through whatever unresolved issues exist. I've found the technique to be a very powerful tool, especially for people dealing with grief and loss issues. But, it does require imagination and a certain degree of risk-taking on the part of the client, a risk some clients feel awkward or silly taking. After all, as therapists we're asking them to "play act" with us, and some adults find that feels childish and uncomfortable for them.

Mattie was one of those people, at first anyway. When I described the empty chair process to her, she leveled a skeptical gaze at me and said, "This is no joking matter, doctor." But, when I was able to persuade her to at least give it a try, we were both pleased at how well it worked for her. Putting a photo of Avery against the back of the empty chair helped her get started. Once we did that, she took a long moment to really stare at the photo, and her eyes soon welled up, before she had even said one word.

"Oh, baby . . ." she finally began. "What have you gotten yourself into now?" Mattie went on to tell Avery how much she loved him and missed him, how much they all did. She shared memories from his early years, when he was the brightest, funniest, most likable kid anywhere he went. "*Everybody* loved you, baby . . . your teachers, your classmates, the neighbors. If I went to the store without you, people would come up and ask me, 'Where's that precious boy today?' If you could just have steered clear of the drugs . . ."

She had more trouble once she got to talking to him about his teen and young adult years, but she forged on bravely. "What I never got is why you'd want to *escape* that way. You had it all, son . . . friends, girls hanging on you, family that would do anything in the world for you. Why wasn't that enough? Why'd you have to run away into drugs and liquor?"

Finally, she seemed spent. "I don't know what to do now, honey. People want me to have a service for you. It just doesn't feel right yet, but I figure I'll know when it's time. Maybe you can give me some sort of sign." She lapsed into silence there.

After a respectful pause, I told Mattie that she'd done a

wonderful piece of work just then, and she smiled. "Especially for someone who thought it was a silly idea, huh?"

"Well, there is that," I had to agree.

In the weeks ahead, Mattie continued to do some empty chair work in our sessions, but also branched out into other therapeutic modalities, including journaling and dream analysis. She had a vivid imagination and brought in wonderful, moving passages from her journals that she read to me in sessions, mainly letters she'd written to Avery telling him her thoughts and feelings about his absence from her life, but also recordings of her dreams, which were colorful, fanciful, and sometimes disturbing. In one particularly happy one, she was riding with him on a merry-go-round at an amusement park, something he had loved to do as a youngster she told me, only they were both adults in this dream, surrounded by little children on the ride. In another, she was rowing a boat alone on the river, and was horrified when one of her oars bumped into something in the water, and she looked down to see Avery's body bobbing on the surface.

Through these activities, Mattie seemed to be getting stronger every time I saw her. In one session, she brought her daughter Denise with her because Denise wanted to share her wishes for her mom's recovery with me.

"Doctor, we've *got* to have some sort of a service for our brother," Denise told me. "People are asking for it and talking about us for not doing something already. They're saying it's not respectful, and we must not have cared much about him because we haven't sent him off yet."

"I *told* you," Mattie said through pursed lips. "We'll do it when it's *time* and only *I* get to say when it's time."

Denise threw me a look appealing for support, but I had to

agree with her mother. "I'm sorry, Denise, but I think your mom is right. What does it matter what people say, after all? It's your family's private matter and others have no right to judge you."

"Huh!" Denise grunted. "They may have no right but they're doing it anyway."

Based on the way that session ended, I figured it could still be a long while before Mattie was ready for a memorial service for Avery. But she proved me wrong in our next session.

"I think I've gotten my sign," she began the session that day. "I've had another dream, but this one is real different. Someone knocked on my door, and when I went to answer it, Avery was standing there on the stoop. Only it wasn't the Avery that came to my door that last night of his life . . . this was the old Avery, cocky and handsome and full of himself, just looking at me like he was glad to see me, and smiling that beautiful smile he used to have. I started to tell him how glad I was to see him, how glad I was that he was alive after all, but he smiled and shook his head, almost like he was shushing me . . . and then he just faded away."

I had to agree with Mattie that this seemed to be a very important dream indeed. "So what do you think it means?" I asked.

She drew a deep breath. "That he's happy wherever he is, and it's time for me to let him go. I'm ready to have the service."

Mattie had finally moved beyond her denial, bargaining, anger, and depression and entered the bittersweet stage of acceptance. I say "bittersweet" here because there's usually little to celebrate about reaching resignation; we're still missing our lost loved one, and wishing they were here with us. But, there in our new state of acceptance, the heart is so much calmer, and the mind is so much more peaceful. We're done at last with all the emotional turmoil and angst. We've finally come to terms with the idea that death comes for all of us, and we've reached some degree of serenity about that.

Mattie spent the rest of that session envisioning what she wanted the service to look like, and by the time we ended, she had a plan for the whole event. She wanted it to be a quiet memorial attended just by family and close friends who would reminisce about the good times in Avery's life.

The next time I saw Mattie, the service had indeed occurred and she was full of stories to share about it. But, as often happens in life, sometimes our plans don't work out, yet the outcome is better than what we'd originally intended. Turns out, word of the service had spread far and wide, and more people had come to it than Mattie had wanted. Unable to turn them away, she had let the crowd grow until it filled the church. Then, as the event unfolded, and speaker after speaker took to the podium, she heard about a far different Avery than the drug-addicted derelict of the last few years.

The crowd laughed often, she recalled, as friends told tales about Avery's mischievous sense of humor, and his charming way with the girls. Some of those same girls drew tears from the gathering as they remembered sweet things he had said and done for them. By the end of the service, when a strong alto soloist sang "Amazing Grace" a capella, there wasn't a dry eye in the house. Clearly, Mattie knew now, though Avery had ended his life as a very troubled young man, he also had a lot of friends and family who had loved him dearly in spite of his problems, and who would miss him terribly for a long time to come.

Mattie would continue to come see me for several follow-up visits after the service for Avery. But, the tone and content of her conversations with me changed noticeably following the memorial. She seemed far more relaxed, far less bitter and angry. She still talked often about her "baby boy," but in a fond, nostalgic way now, rather than the angry, guilt-ridden way she had before. Finally, she told me she thought she was ready to take a break from therapy, for the time being at least.

"The Reverend has me running all over the place taking care of kids and old people," she laughed. "I just don't have time for this therapy stuff right now!"

We agreed she would come in as-needed from that point, and she hasn't been back to see me since. She, her family, and her community sent Avery's spirit to rest in a powerful, healing experience, so I doubted she would be haunted by painful memories again.

Mattie's story reminds us of some very important ideas about grieving and healing the loss of a loved one, especially an adult child. The first is that grieving has no formulaic process or schedule; it's a deeply personal journey that each individual has to accomplish on their own terms and timeline. "Only *I* get to say when it's time," Mattie had insisted to her daughter Denise, and she was right to do so to protect her need to grieve as she saw fit.

The second idea is that "closure," such a nice, resonant word and concept, can't be guaranteed by any particular steps or events; we each need to find it in our own special way. For many, closure comes through a combination of time, prayer, support from family and friends, and healing rituals, such as funerals, memorial services, erecting headstones at gravesites, or scattering loved ones' ashes after cremations. But, there is no guidebook for how to achieve closure, and the best thing family, friends, and therapists can offer grieving parents is an open mind and a willing ear; we need to just *listen* to them and support them any way we can in finding their way through that dark forest.

Finally, Mattie teaches us that one of the best ways to heal our own pain is to reach out to others, especially people experiencing other kinds of pain, and try to help them. It's hard to feel sorry for yourself and ruminate on your own suffering when you're feeding a homeless child, or serving lunch at a soup kitchen filled with tired street people. And it's precisely because Mattie had become so immersed in her lay ministry under Reverent Steven's tutelage that I doubted I'd ever hear from her again. The last time I saw her she was a woman on a mission, and people with that kind of "fire in their belly" usually don't need much help from a therapist.

Suggestions for Further Reading and Learning

In this chapter, I've already referenced one of the most important resources concerning grief and loss issues ever developed, Elizabeth Kubler-Ross's *On Death and Dying*, which has been revised and reprinted several times over the years since its original publication. Kubler-Ross's work in this landmark book is seminal and despite the fact that numerous other fine books on the mourning process exist, I can't honestly recommend anything else to readers that improves on it. However, I can suggest another important resource for parents grieving the loss of an adult child, the nationwide support group Compassionate Friends, which I already alluded to in earlier chapters. For information about where to find the nearest group, readers should call their local community mental health center information line.

CHAPTER 10

Special Issues and Needs When Parents or Adult Children Are Gay

Or, "Teaching others how to treat us"

F ew social issues have received more attention in recent years than the issue of gay rights. While several presidents, federal and state legislatures, and all branches of the military have struggled with the unpopular, "Don't ask, don't tell" policy, the American public has expressed divided sentiments. Many people argue for gay rights, while others eschew them as special treatment not guaranteed by the Constitution.

In the midst of this contentious social discourse, countless human stories have fallen between the cracks. As the national debate continues, gay parents and children have struggled with questions about how to be the best family they can be to each other. Recognizing that, like it or not, homosexuality is a part of their lives, they try hard to figure out what kind of energy and attention they should give to it.

One of the most interesting and rewarding aspects of my work with clients in this arena is that I have been able to counsel both gay parents and gay adult children, thus gleaning insights from both perspectives. The following case histories recount some of those experiences.

Starting with the parents' perspective, I find myself thinking first of Roland Nabb. A handsome, dignified, middle-aged man, Roland was the father of a pretty, vivacious twenty-two-year-old daughter, Brett. Roland grew up in the coal-mining country of Eastern Kentucky, in a world where life was hard, money was scarce, and church was often a fundamentalist, fire-and-brimstone experience. His father was a coal miner and farmer, and the family just barely kept food on the table and clothes on their backs through most of Roland's childhood. An apt student, Roland had won scholarships to college and had actually finished *several* master's degrees, the first in his family to do so.

Like many people who wonder about their sexual orientation as teenagers, Roland had tried to be heterosexual, finding and falling in love with Sally, a pretty, winsome classmate from Sunday school at the Pentecostal Church he attended. They had married and he had even become a minister of the church himself for a time.

Playing house successfully in those early days, Roland and Sally soon had a daughter. But, not long after delivering, Sally had pulled away from Roland, devoting herself totally to caring for the baby and denying him sex.

Being a young virile man, Rowland now found himself in an unusual situation. He had very strong feelings of attraction for men, and though he had never really acted on them, he had "played around a little." Surprisingly, he found that he never had to wander far to get his needs met, despite being a director of music in his church and a national officer in the Southern Baptist Convention.

"I'll never forget when the pastor, a good-looking young man, and I were on our way to Atlanta for a national convention and he looked me in the eye and said 'You know, I think most ministers are either crazy or gay . . . which one are you?' I can honestly say that I've had more sex with closeted married church leaders than I have with other gay men since I moved to Louisville to be with my true love!"

"And the rest is history," he laughed in our first session. "I've been an openly gay man for decades now and I've never looked back."

Fortunately for him, Roland had found Kiernan, a successful builder and the love of his life, shortly after divorcing Sally and coming out. He had moved to Louisville to be with Kiernan, where he had also found an important, high-paying job in city government. He continued to go back to Eastern Kentucky to see Brett as often as possible. But, little by little, Roland's world began to be centered more in Louisville than in Eastern Kentucky. By the time Brett was a teenager, she had definitely grown apart from her dad, cleaving more to the values of her mother, an embittered woman who still embraced the rigid doctrine of the Pentecostal faith. Things got even worse when Roland's ex-wife remarried, a man whom Brett loved and came to call "Dad."

"I almost lost her for good," Roland reminisced with me, looking back on that time. "Brett and I went years without talking to or seeing each other when she was a teen. Oh, I tried to keep the lines of communication open with cards and gifts. But sometimes she didn't even acknowledge having gotten my presents. She was one angry little girl in those days."

Just about the time Roland had accepted the idea he might

have to give up on all hopes for a relationship with his daughter, things took an unexpected turn. Brett called him one night to tell him that she was engaged to be married, and to ask him to help her plan her wedding. She also wanted Kiernan to plan and orchestrate all the "high church" music, including hiring musicians and soloists.

"Guess she figured out sometimes a gal needs a good 'queen' to help her make major fashion decisions," he laughed, remembering that call. And of course, Roland was there for his daughter totally as the big day approached, guiding her every step along the way, advising and supporting and mentoring her in each decision.

He spent hours making hand-made mints and chocolate baskets for hundreds of guests. And of course, she had to have just the right shade of periwinkle tablecloths, so not being able to find the exact color she wanted, he made all the tablecloths, too.

In the biggest challenge of all for him, Brett had even asked Roland to make her wedding cake, for he was an accomplished baker whose work had won several awards over the years at the Kentucky State Fair.

"How I labored over that masterpiece," he recalled, a wistful smile on his face. "I hand-made and painted all the icing flowers on the cake, Asiatic lilies, they were, and it took over forty hours just for that part. I couldn't use my fingers for days! But it's amazing what you'll do for your little angel, and it was probably my best work ever, if I do say so myself."

Finally, the big day arrived and Roland and Kiernan loaded up the cake, and headed to Eastern Kentucky to support Brett in the most important event of her life so far.

"I guess I should have seen it coming, but I didn't," Roland said, remembering that day, one of the worst days of his life. "I knew something was wrong the moment we arrived. Kiernan and I were struggling to get that blasted cake into the church reception hall without dropping it, and no one even came out to greet us or help us. We finally made it inside and got the cake set up on the banquet table, but still no sign of Brett or anyone else for that matter."

Roland went on to tell one of the most heartbreaking stories I think I've ever heard from a client. "When we finally did track down Brett, she was anxious and stressed. There were problems with her gown not fitting and they had summoned a seamstress to fix it. She begged off talking to me for the time and I took that in stride."

What Roland didn't see coming was a development that proved to be the most wounding experience he'd ever had as a parent. As the service was about to begin, Roland asked the wedding planner where he should stand in order to intercept Brett to walk her down the aisle.

"Oh, that won't be necessary," the planner told him. "Brett's stepfather will be doing that."

Roland was devastated. "I don't think I've ever been more hurt in my whole life," he told me. "But this was her day, after all, not mine and I didn't want to do anything to spoil it for her."

So, Roland did his best to do the noble, adult thing, sitting in a front pew, watching Brett walk down the aisle with her stepfather instead of him. "All the while, Kiernan was taking care of the music, making sure it was the most beautiful wedding possible," he recalled. "He had no idea I was sitting in the front pew trying to hold myself together and not walk out!"

Despite everything, Roland still managed to find it a beautiful service and a wonderful moment. "I was able to get into the spirit of the thing and let go of any resentments or hurt feelings I was experiencing at the time."

That charm only lasted so long. The spell evaporated once the reception began and Brett continued to avoid her father. "Every time I got anywhere near her, someone needed a photo of her with someone else and whisked her off. No one ever suggested a photo of her with me."

It was now abundantly clear to Roland that he was being snubbed at his only daughter's wedding because he was gay, a wedding he had helped planned and baked the wedding cake for. "Of course the main thing I felt was an overwhelming *rage*," he recalled. "But that was just a defense against the incredible hurt and sadness. It occurred to me that maybe I didn't really know my little girl at all anymore . . . that during all those years apart from me under her mother's thumb she had grown into a stranger, someone I didn't even want to know."

Still, he struggled with what to do about the present dilemma. "I'm not one to cause public scenes," he admitted. "But then, Brett knew that, and it struck me that maybe she was counting on my good manners to let her get away with the mean and sneaky thing she was doing just then."

He broke into a big grin that belied the tears in his eyes. "So, I let her have it!" he crowed. "I walked into the middle of the room and literally *bellowed* her name. The silence was deafening, but I had her attention at last. 'Hope you enjoy the cake I baked for you because I won't be around to see you cut it,' I said. Then she looked me straight in the eye and said, 'Please, just leave my wedding!' And with that I made the grandest exit you ever saw!"

Roland clearly took pleasure in the memory, but admitted it

was a hollow victory in many ways. "I could never have lived with myself if I'd let her treat me so shabbily. But that just widened the gulf between us. It would be years before Brett and I spoke again."

As it turned out, once again a major life milestone would bring Brett back into Roland's life. "I almost couldn't believe my eyes when I got a big fat envelope from her one day," he told me. "Inside was the most abject apology I think I've ever gotten. She was pregnant with her first baby, and she'd realized she couldn't bring this child into a world without a relationship with his '*real* grandpa.' Well, I totally broke down and cried forever. But when I was through, I called her up and we talked for hours, clearing the air, and catching up and imagining all kinds of wonderful things we were going to do together with the baby. And we've been close ever since."

While Roland's story had a happy ending, I had to admit to him that I would have never seen that coming, after he had been betrayed so badly by Brett's behavior at her wedding. I've counseled many clients over the years who became estranged from family completely and permanently, over far less hurtful actions. But Roland had a huge heart and a forgiving nature. "And besides," he added. "That little boy is the center of my universe, and I'm the center of his. When he comes running to me and calls me 'Papa Nabb' my heart just melts."

Roland's experience reminded me of the old saying, "We teach others how to treat us," a truism for which I have "love-hate feelings." Taken too literally, it can leave us feeling responsible for the harmful things others do to us, which are sometimes actually beyond our control. On the other hand, when others do hurt us, we can often look back and see that there were things we could have done to make them respect us more and treat us better. That was very much the case with Roland Nabb.

Remembering Brett's total absence during her teenaged years, he had jumped at the chance to restore their relationship through helping her with her wedding. However, looking back, he could identify all kinds of warning signs that all was not as it should be. "That little girl can be a *spoiled brat* sometimes!" he said, recounting shopping trips and conferences with the wedding planner where Brett was impatient and demanding, throwing tantrums if anyone suggested any idea she didn't like. "I was embarrassed to be seen with her," he admitted. "And I should have realized then that she was selfish enough to do whatever it took to have things her way, including not having to deal with her gay father on her wedding day."

In *Codependent No More*, Melody Beattie makes some wonderful suggestions for how to get our life and self-respect back when we've made the mistake of becoming enmeshed with and hurt by unhealthy relationships in our lives. The first step in this healing process is to acknowledge the painful truth that the relationship is unhealthy, and identify the ways that it's harmful to us. Having gained that insight, we can then set more effective boundaries on the harmful aspects of the relationship, and begin to detach emotionally from it. In the process, we begin to rebuild our sense of self-reliance and self-respect.

To recover from his formerly codependent relationship with Brett, Roland had to first admit that what she was doing to him at her wedding was mean-spirited and disrespectful. Then, after confronting her, he had remove himself from the hurtful situation, maintaining his silence and distance until she was able to grow up enough to acknowledge and apologize for her wrongdoing.

Another important aspect of Roland's recovery was his being willing to "make a scene." It's been my experience with clients involved in unhealthy relationships that they often try to smooth things over and avoid surfacing open conflict. In the process, they may inadvertently enable others to bully them, and can lose their self-respect and personal integrity along the way.

In numerous works dealing with conflict resolution, author David Johnson talks about the importance of facing and managing conflict through creative problem-solving strategies. Admittedly, he says, there are times when conflict avoidance is the wisest approach, such as when violence is possible. But generally, he concludes conflict avoidance just exacerbates problems. And Roland was able to admit that his placating of Brett's willfulness in the months before her wedding had actually set him up for the hurt she eventually caused him.

Roland wasn't alone in this respect. Over the years, countless gay clients have shared similar stories with me concerning the important lessons they've learned about the role of self-respect in fostering healthy relationships with others in their lives, especially heterosexual family and friends, and especially during their coming-out experiences. Living in a heterosexist and homophobic world that often denies gay people's very humanity, gay people need to work extra hard to value themselves, and show others they expect respect and fair treatment. That was the difficult lesson another client, Chuck Best, learned in coming out to his parents.

Chuck was a tall and lanky self-professed "old hippie," who

worked days as a "cable guy" and played keyboard at nights in a local rock band. "We're not very good, but we 'make a joyful noise' that people seem to like," he told me in our first session.

He originally sought treatment with me for depression after a painful break-up with an abusive former partner. He had actually been hospitalized on several occasions for the injuries this partner inflicted on him, and it was there that hospital staff had linked him up with an expert on domestic violence who advised him for the first time that he was a classic victim of spouse abuse.

"I didn't much care for the label," he told me. "But after I heard the traits, I had to admit it fit me." Over time, Chuck had come to believe his abuser's assertions that he brought the abuse on himself and even deserved it. He had tried to keep the peace by avoiding conflict, walking on eggshells, and denying his own needs. Nevertheless, none of these efforts worked, as is always true in domestic violence situations, because the violence originates within the perpetrator's own maladaptive personality and inability to engage in mutual, loving relationships. So, no matter what Chuck did to try to avoid angering his partner, the partner always found some reason to vent his spleen on Chuck.

Chuck finally got out with the help of the domestic violence specialists at Louisville's Center for Women and Families. Unfortunately, there is no agency in the region that specializes in working with gay and lesbian abuse victims, but in the absence of such an agency, the Center for Women and Families does a fine job of serving this population. In the process, Chuck also had to move in with his parents, because he had nowhere else to go, and no funds to rent a place of his own.

While living with his parents, Chuck had to deal with their constant questions about his love life, or rather the lack of it, and why he never brought any girls home to meet them. He had always portrayed his partner as his "roommate" to them, and they had no idea he was gay. He had lied about the injuries that put him in the hospital, saying he had fallen down the stairs, so his parents also had no idea that he was a domestic violence survivor. The truth about everything emerged when a well-meaning, but tactless, friend came to visit Chuck and blew the whole story in his folks' earshot.

"You never should have shacked up with that creep," the friend had chastised Chuck, not realizing that his parents were in the next room, and that Chuck had never come out to them. "No matter how much you loved him. I always knew he was bad news."

After the friend left, Chuck's parents came to him and asked "Is it true?" He admitted to them that yes, it was, but was unprepared for their response. "They called their minister, made an emergency appointment for the three of us, and dragged me off to see this guy about joining an ex-gay recovery program!"

The ex-gay ministries movement is one that has experienced several name changes and developmental hiccups over the years, not just in the Louisville area, but across the nation. Its basic tenets are the same, no matter what it's called or where it surfaces: homosexuality is a sin and abomination that only Christ can cure, and only by embracing Him as our personal savior can we be saved from it. Ex-gay ministers are often "former" gay people themselves who profess to have been saved from the lifestyle, although in a curious contradiction to this assertion, they normally practice paired with a heterosexual partner who ensures that nothing inappropriate happens between them and their gay clients.

Knowing all of this, Chuck resisted talking to the pastor and getting involved with the whole ex-gay recovery program. "But I was living with my folks who had taken me in to help me and they hit me in a weak spot. I know they love me and I know they love their church. They really believe this stuff and it's their *whole life*. I didn't have the heart to say no to them."

The "weak spot" Chuck was referring to was his own internalized homophobia, a term used to describe the fear of being homosexual that gay people "catch" from the heterosexual world that surrounds them. In the throes of this internalized homophobia, gay people often deny or try to suppress their true identity and feelings. They may indulge in making jokes about gay people, or in extreme cases, even oppress other gay people while pretending to be straight themselves.

Chuck's particular brand of internalized homophobia manifested in a willingness to try the ex-gay recovery program for his parents' sake, despite knowing it would never work, and despite hating the idea of participating in it. But to please his folks, he began seeing a "counselor-couple" at a local mega-church known for its ex-gay ministries. Almost immediately, he began to suffer a serious depression. By the time he had scheduled his first appointment with me, he was contemplating suicide.

"I mean, what kind of life is this I'm fighting for, after all?" he mused that first day. "My folks hate my 'being this way' . . . the man I loved more than anyone in the whole world beat the crap out of me because he hates both of us for 'being this way' . . . and I took all of that abuse from him because I thought I deserved it for 'being this way.'

Maybe I just *shouldn't* 'be this way,' or if I can't change it, maybe I just shouldn't be here *at all* anymore."

Chuck had reached the point where the very thought of pursuing the rest of his life as an openly gay man seemed so dismal that he was actually considering ending it. Clearly he needed some form of "shock therapy" to jolt him out of this self-destructive mind set. Normally I'm extremely risk averse in dealing with my clients, avoiding techniques that are confrontational or provocative in any way, especially with clients who are suicidal. People in that fragile and vulnerable mind set need total support and tried-and-true clinical interventions from their therapist. But something about Chuck's hippie persona and creative spirit suggested to me that I might be safe in trying something a little different with him.

"So okay," I began. "Let's do *It's a Wonderful Life* together. What would the world be like without Chuck Best in it anymore?"

He threw me a startled look and then broke into a wry smile. "Good question," he said. Then he sobered a bit and seemed to give the matter some serious consideration. "Well, for starters the band would fold. To tell the truth, we really kinda suck. Not to brag, but I'm the only real musician in the lot."

"And all those people who like the joyful noise you make?" I asked.

He grinned. "Guess they'll have to find some other bad band to follow."

We went on in this playful way for several minutes, imagining all the people Chuck knew whose world would be better or worse off without him in it. Then something in the process took a turn for him and his eyes welled with tears. "I don't really want to die," he whispered, burying his face in his hands. "I just don't want to go on the way I have been anymore!" Here at last was Chuck's teachable moment.

"So, what do you want to change?" I asked and was relieved to see him look up with a determined look in his eyes.

"I don't ever want to have to lie about *anything* anymore," he said. "Not who I am, or what I do, or what I want out of life, especially love from another man."

"And how are you going to get there?" I asked, glad once more to see the growing resolve in his face.

"Not by going to ex-gay counseling," he said. "And not by living with my parents. No matter how much I know they love me, it can't change the fact that they hate who I am and what I stand for. I hope I never have to cut them out of my life or they have to cut me out of theirs. But, we can't really be 'friends' as long as they believe that *who I truly am*, is wrong. Guess it's time to get my own place, one way or another, huh?"

As often happens with my clients, Chuck had just answered his own question, realizing how to alleviate his depression and begin a whole new chapter in his life by claiming his true self and striking out on his own.

There would be plenty of other challenges for him in the months ahead. He would rent and subsequently lose a wonderful loft apartment in a trendy neighborhood of Old Louisville after he was laid off from his day job. He would argue with his parents and quit speaking to them for a while when they pressured him to return to the Ex-Gay Program. He would find several boyfriends online, date them for a while, then break up with each of them, once he realized they weren't what he was looking for in a man. But throughout all of these challenges, Chuck would never consider suicide again.

* * *

So, in closing this discussion, a question goes begging: what is it about the curious condition of being gay that causes such conflict for so many people, both gay and straight? I can't help but feel that the heart of the matter is this: being gay just isn't what most of us saw modeled at home growing up. How many of us knew gay couples when we were children? By far, most of us saw only heterosexual couples as the norm. And by the very lack of gay role models in our early world, many of us have been disadvantaged in learning how to love our true selves and each other, not *in spite of* but *because of* being gay.

Fortunately, better times are here now for gay youth and young adults in many cities, thanks to support groups like the Louisville Youth Group for gay and lesbian teens. As a former board member for this group, I was often touched to see how much more self-aware and self-respecting the kids who attended this group were than my peers and I were at the same age. To their advantage, these youth have grown up in a world where television shows and movies frequently include gay characters, some of which may not be the greatest role models, but at least they're *there* in the broader social landscape that modern youth survey, rather than an invisible demographic group whose existence no one ever acknowledges.

Certainly contemporary American culture still has a long way to go toward fully accepting and affirming sexual diversity. Crimes such as the Matthew Shepard murder still occur throughout the country, though at lower frequencies, thanks to the statutes many communities have passed outlawing hate crimes. Yet within individual families, such as Roland Nabb's and Chuck Best's, being a gay parent or adult child is still fraught with special challenges. I look forward to the time when that landscape changes as well.

Suggestions for Further Reading and Learning

Readers wanting to understand better what it means to be a gay or lesbian parent or child in modern American culture will find the following resources helpful:

Downs, A. *The Velvet Rage: Overcoming the Pain of Growing Up Gay in a Straight Man's World*. Cambridge, MA: DeCapo Lifelong Books, 2005.

Kooden, H. and Flowers, C. *Golden Men: The Power of Gay Mid-life*. New York, NY: Avon Books, 2000.

Isay, T. *Becoming Gay: The Journey to Self-Acceptance*. New York, NY: Henry Holt and Company, 1996.

Reed, R. *Growing Up Gay*. New York, NY: W.W. Norton, 1997.

Tobias, A. *The Best Little Boy in the World Grows Up*. New York, NY: Ballantine Books, 1998.

In addition, readers may find it helpful to visit a meeting of Parents and Friends of Lesbians and Gays (PFLAG). To find out where PFLAG meetings occur, readers should contact their nearest community mental health center.

CHAPTER 11

The Adult Child's Perspective

Or, "What I Need from You, Mom and Dad"

No discussion about parenting adult children would be complete without considering the child's perspective. In the preceding case scenarios, I've tried to focus at least some attention on the issues and needs of the adult children involved in each case, though admittedly that attention was largely from the parents' viewpoint. The following case scenario focuses strictly on the adult child's viewpoint.

As we've already seen many times in earlier chapters, few adult children are totally independent from their parents, even when they may be largely autonomous and self-sufficient from them. Complex psychological, emotional, and social needs often exist, even in children who are financially and physically self-reliant. Angela Manning's grown children all had successful careers, comfortable homes, and solid relationships with significant others, but they still needed their mom to baby-sit and treat them to dinners or shows from time to time. Roland Nabb's daughter had a loving husband, a good job, and a happy, growing family, but she still needed him to be a *"real* grandfather;" the stepfather she called "Dad" just couldn't fill that role.

We've already seen several adult children who relied solely on their parents' financial and physical support, literally needing to live with their parents, and have them provide groceries, clothes, and other necessities. As a result, the following case study deals mainly with the psychological, emotional, and social needs referenced above.

What are some of the specific things in these areas that adult children need from their parents? Here's what my clients have expressed to me:

- Ongoing emotional support and affirmation;
- Mentoring about how to manage special life challenges;
- Achieving healing and closure for old childhood wounds;
- Permission to be their true self without parents' judgment or disapproval;
- Role modeling on how to grow older with dignity and grace;
- Opportunities to share fun as two adults with shared interests and histories;
- Candid guidance about parents' end-of-life wishes.

Forty-five-year-old Trent Culbertson's story addressed each and every one of these needs. I first met him when he was referred to me for counseling through the employee assistance program at his workplace, a large law firm in downtown Louisville, where he was employed as a paralegal.

Trent was going through a difficult time in his marriage following a brief affair he had with Janice, a woman he had met on an out-of-town business trip. She had become pregnant and wanted to keep the baby. She had contacted Trent to ask for his support, which he had committed to her, and he had subsequently felt the need to tell his wife Anita the whole story.

"Anita's an amazing woman," he told me in that first session. "She actually told me I'd done the right thing to agree to support Janice and the baby. Oh, she cried for sure, and still isn't sure what she wants to do with our marriage. But, I hope she'll decide to give me another chance." Trent did indeed seem to be a lucky man in many ways, despite the fact that he had gotten a woman other than his wife pregnant, and was now uncertain about the future of his marriage

As I got to know more about his background, I learned that Trent had actually had a very colorful life in many ways. He described himself as an "Army brat" recounting how his father, Trent Senior, had been a career military man. His father had done active duty in three wars, including World War II, Korea, and Vietnam, and earned the rank of colonel. Trent's pride was obvious as he talked about his dad's service, and how he and his mother had traveled the world following his dad from post to post.

Eventually they settled down in Louisville when his dad retired, and his mother had gotten an important job as an administrative assistant to the CEO of a worldwide corporation headquartered here. Trent's pride in his mother's success may have been even greater than his pride in his dad's, as he confided that his relationship with his mom had always been especially close, due to the long periods of separation they experienced from his dad when he was stationed elsewhere.

Despite his clear love and admiration for his father, Trent shared that they had always struggled in their relationship with each other. His dad tended to be something of a martinet at home, expecting his household and family life to function like life on an Army base. Trent could laugh now at old memories of his dad coming home and barking orders like he was commanding his men about on the battlefield.

"But, it also hurt a lot," he added. "To never feel like things were good enough to please him, not me, not mom, not the way we lived at home."

Things eventually became strained enough between his dad and mom that they actually separated and divorced for a time. "That was a tough spell for sure," Trent recalled with me. "I was just a kid at the time, but I felt like I had to be the man of the house and take care of my mother."

Fortunately, he was able to add, that difficult chapter in the family's life didn't last long. His parents were miserable without each other and remarried less than two years later, at which time his father retired, and the family moved to Louisville. Trent attended the best Catholic male high school in the region, and graduated with honors, though not without his dad pressing him to always do even better. Things would become even more strained between Trent and his dad once he graduated from high school.

"Dad couldn't afford to pay my way through college on a soldier's retirement income, so I decided to go into the service myself and get my tuition paid that way." The only problem was Trent had no interest in going into the Army. He wanted to go sign up with the Air Force instead. "You'd have thought I was joining the Communist Party from Dad's reaction to that decision!"

As a result, the two strong-willed men went through the first of several estrangements they would experience throughout the years ahead. Things took an unexpected turn for the better when Trent "finally did something right in Dad's eyes," becoming engaged to Anita. Trent met Anita in the Air Force where she was also in service, and his dad absolutely adored her from the moment he first saw her.

"Anita brought us all back together again," he recalled. "Or I should say she and mom did, working as a team."

The young couple married, and began their lives as another military family. The following year they had their first and only child, a daughter, "Marty" short for Martha, named after Trent's mom. They were happy, Trent remembered, despite going through some of the common struggles most young couples face, especially those serving in the military. At times, they were stationed apart and had to endure long separations. But their daughter thrived, growing into a smart, cheerful, and beautiful little girl. Her granddad adored her as much, if not more than he did her mother.

Then an unfortunate accident sidelined Anita's career. She was involved in a car accident, and experienced severe injuries to her back that would require numerous surgeries and painful rounds of physical therapy for years to come. She opted for an honorable discharge for medical reasons and became a full-time mom and homemaker for a while.

Fast forward several years. Trent was now retired from the Air Force as well, and worked as a paralegal in Louisville. He found it challenging, but interesting too, for the most part. Anita had finished her business degree and gone to work as a manager in a large local company that manufactured medical equipment. Marty was now an honor student in one of the best Catholic girls' high schools in Louisville. "Life seemed really sweet for a while there," Trent remembered. "Then I messed it all up getting Janice pregnant."

In our early work together, Trent and I mainly focused on getting him through the difficult time of indecision about the future of his marriage. The couple had long, heartfelt talks together at home, and Anita even joined us at my office for some marital sessions. Trent wrote her long, loving letters recalling all the good times in their marriage and begging her for forgiveness and the chance to start again. But ultimately his efforts failed. Anita couldn't get past the hurt she felt over Trent's infidelity, and though she admitted to still loving him, she couldn't continue to be married to him.

Naturally, Trent was devastated by her decision. Though he took full responsibility for his own mistakes, he had hoped against hope that Anita would ultimately forgive him. Now that she had made clear she wanted out of the marriage, he had no more hope to sustain him and fell into a deep depression. I worried about his safety a lot in those days, as he struggled with suicidal thoughts and saw no reason to go on living without the love of his life, Anita. He had reached the lowest ebb of any client I've ever worked with, when yet another instance of bad luck took him even deeper into despair, something I hadn't thought possible.

One night soon after Anita's decision, Trent called me from the hospital where his mother had just been taken with a heart attack. "I just can't lose Mom, too," he sobbed. "She was always my biggest supporter and fan. Now that Anita's leaving me, I just can't go on without Mom."

But fate wasn't going to let Trent have any respite. His mother died that night with the whole family gathered around her bedside. The only blessing to be found in this tragedy was that

Anita delayed her decision to leave Trent, and committed to stay with him for a time to help him to deal with his mother's death.

The next time I saw him for a session, Trent had rallied enough that he was actually able to quip with me a bit. "You know how I keep saying *now* I've *really* hit rock bottom, so the good news it can't get any worse than this?" he asked. When I nodded yes, he went on. "Well, you gotta stop me from saying that anymore, because *every time I say it, things do get worse!*"

As time went by, another unexpected and bittersweet development would occur. Something about losing his wife of sixty years brought Trent Senior to a new appreciation of the importance of family, and especially the importance of a positive relationship with his son. Trent shared with me in sessions how his father seemed to have softened somehow. His dad called him more often and seemed to be making an effort to be less judgmental and critical.

"Oh, he can still get on my very last nerve with one of his 'you oughta do this better' comments," Trent sighed. "But he makes them less often and I think I can see him trying to hold his tongue some times."

In the weeks and months ahead, Trent would continue to experience one of the worst strings of bad luck I've ever seen any client undergo. He lost his job at the law firm, had to file for bankruptcy, and learned that Janice was pregnant with twins. Anita finally moved out, taking Marty with her, leaving Trent alone in an empty house. But, throughout this difficult time, his dad stood beside him, calling him up and inviting him to come play cards, watch a movie, or go out to dinner together.

"Sometimes I want to ask him 'what planet did you just

come down from and what have you done with my *real* dad?'"
he joked in one of our sessions. But, it was also apparent that
Trent treasured this new relationship with his dad, and enjoyed
his time together with the old man tremendously. His father
had even begun sharing anecdotes with him about his life, his
career, his marriage, and his memories of Trent's early days,
recalling experiences from those times that Trent had never
heard about.

Gradually Trent began to see that his dad wanted to reflect
with him about his own life and their life together, a process
that some developmental psychologists refer to as a "life review,"
brought on by the awareness of aging. Rather than pontificating
about what Trent ought to be doing differently with his life, his
dad just wanted to share time and memories with him. In these
dialogues, Trent learned that he was more like his dad than
he would have ever been able to admit once upon a time. The
two men were even able to share some laughs about that fact,
helping Trent to feel that his dad had finally accepted him fully
and unequivocally for the person that he was—like his dad in
some ways but very unlike him in others. He also saw his dad,
now a very old man of eighty-five, actually maturing in new
ways, and becoming wiser and gentler as he neared the end of
his own life.

Through his dad's role modeling and mentoring in those
days, Trent came to see aging and death not as something to be
resisted and feared, but something natural and even good about
the human condition. He certainly enjoyed all kinds of emotional
support and affirmation from his dad, as well as help achieving
closure to their old relationship struggles. He felt that his dad
was trying to show him the path to a different way of doing life,

taking its troubles in stride, and facing aging with dignity and grace. He was also able to have "just some plain old fun" with his dad, as they bickered in those visits over card games, ball games, and political matters.

As often happens when elderly men lose their wives, Trent Senior's own health began to fail not long after Martha died. A lifetime smoker, he was diagnosed with chronic obstructive pulmonary disease, and went in and out of the hospital several times with life-threatening bouts of pneumonia. Trent and Anita were divorced by then and he had moved to Wisconsin to be with Janice and the twins she had recently delivered. He had found work as a manager at a local department store, and was also pursuing courses to become a high school teacher. But, as his father's health faltered, he came home as often as he could to try to be there for the old man in every way possible.

Finally in one of these last visits, Trent Senior looked at the minister who had come by to pray with him, and his son sitting at his bedside. Pointing to the ceiling, he said simply, "Time to go home and see Martha again." He would die later that night, and like his wife, he was surrounded by family and friends.

Many modern thanatologists, specialists in death and dying issues, talk about a concept most Americans find to be a mind-blowing oxymoron, "the *good* death." As a society that values being self-reliant, goal-centered, and proactive in every way possible, we just can't seem to come to terms with the fact that we've all got to die someday. So, we pretty up our loved ones' remains and talk about everlasting life at their funerals, all the while indulging in the most complete and total denial imaginable. We just can't seem to deal with the idea that death is a natural part of life, after all. Yet how liberating and inspiring it can be when we see someone face death with acceptance and peace, as Trent Culbertson Senior did.

At Trent's invitation, I attended his father's funeral several days later, and found it to be a beautiful and inspirational memorial. The first thing that struck me as I entered the chapel was how many people were there. It's been my sad observation at the funerals of other elderly people that generally they were small affairs with very few attendees, presumably because many of the deceased person's friends had already died before them. Not so for Colonel Culbertson. The chapel was full, and a military honor guard of handsome, uniformed officers filled the front pew on the right. Trent and Anita and other members of the family occupied the other front pews on the left.

As the prayers were read and the eulogies spoken, it became clear that this was a man who was not only a husband, father, granddad and soldier, but that he had actually been a true war hero. Trent's eulogy was the shortest, but also the more powerful, for in it he acknowledged that he himself hadn't fully realized his father's heroism, but that he did now. What struck me as so powerful about his message was that it expressed what I consider to be an iconic, almost archetypal, human experience. Most of us love our parents, and if we're lucky, we may even truly *like* and enjoy spending time with them.

But, at the day's end, or perhaps I should say at the end of *their* days, many of us discover that maybe we didn't know them as well as we thought we did. Old stories told to us by visitors at viewings or by speakers giving eulogies often contain surprises. We hear anecdotes about events in our parents' lives that they never discussed with us, some funny or touching, others inspiring or hard to believe; "Mom or Dad actually did *that?*" Reading love letters, cards or other documents that we stumble on while sorting through their things, often reveals to us intimate feelings and private moments in their lives that they kept to themselves.

Sometimes, cluttered bureau drawers give up moving mementos from our own lives that we had no idea they'd saved; hand-made gifts, drawings, and cards fashioned with clumsy childish hands, crude in their execution perhaps, but made with love. Trent had found this to be true for him, as well, and he had displayed many such mementos by his father's bier. It seemed to me that he found comfort in explaining to visitors what each of the items was, and its particular significance and history.

Trent honored all of his father's very explicit end-of-life requests. His dad wanted to be buried beside his wife in the plot they had purchased in a beautiful Louisville cemetery. He also wanted everyone to have a big party in his memory, following his funeral, with lots of good food and drink and stories about old memories. Trent made it all happen, once again with Anita's help. They were divorced, but they were still the best of friends who had shared a lifetime together, even if life had taken them down separate paths more recently.

Trent's experiences reminded me of an important truism: no matter how old or how wise or how independent we may come to be as adults in this society, we all need our parents to be there for us to whatever extent they can be. It may be that they're old, disabled or incompetent. But as long as there's breath in their bodies and coherent thinking in their heads, most of us rely on our parents to meet at least some of our needs.

If we all live long enough together, the time will eventually come when we reverse roles with them, and become parents to their increasingly child-like behaviors. But along that road, even though we may pride ourselves on our independence, we still look to mom and dad to reassure ourselves that life is manageable. After all, they had a head start and they made it farther than we have so far, didn't they?

Suggestions for Further Reading and Learning

Several previous chapters have already suggested numerous resources for understanding grief and loss issues. Readers interested in knowing more about end-of-life planning issues will find it helpful to go to the AARP website, and search under the key words "end-of-life planning" or "family issues in end-of-life planning."

CHAPTER 12

The Role of Spirituality in Healing Parent and Adult Child Problems

How looking 'inside' helps us cope with our 'outside'

As we begin to bring this discussion to an end, it's important to remember what we set out to do in the first place. That was to have a dialogue about parenting adult children, by sharing real stories of loving parents and adult children who have turned problems into solutions through their hard work in therapy, and their commitment to each other. Some core principles have guided us along the way.

One principle was the basic assertion that parenting continues far beyond childhood, for as long the parent and child both live, in fact. Another was that parenting children once they become adults may be even more challenging in many ways, because parents have less control and influence over their children then. A final principle was that more needs to be known about parenting adult children, because there's been so little attention to the topic in the media and professional literature, thus far at least.

From there, we set out on a journey to explore helpful strategies for parenting adult children drawn from my casework experiences with clients in my private practice. My clients have learned these lessons for themselves and taught me, as well, making it possible for me to share them with readers in this narrative. Through these clients' sharing, we've wrestled with some weighty challenges:

- Helping overly dependent children grow up and become more independent
- Getting alcohol or drug-addicted children out of the house and into recovery
- Cutting the metaphorical umbilical cord with children who are enmeshed with us by setting better boundaries with them
- Moving from parenting to grandparenting, and avoiding the trap of doing too much for our kids or getting stuck in their life dilemmas
- Recognizing and reversing common projections parents place on their children
- Letting go with serenity when children distance themselves inexplicably
- Understanding the adult child's perspective and need for ongoing support from parents
- Overcoming difficulties that emerge when a child or parent is gay
- Coping when a physically or developmentally challenged child needs care outside the home
- Grieving and healing when a child or parent dies.

In the process of addressing these issues and needs, we met some very strong and admirable people. The strategies they mastered for becoming more effective parents involved a combination of intuition, sensitivity, craft, study, and *luck*. In addition, for most of them, some spiritual growth and healing had to occur; and no, I'm not talking about religion here—far from it, in fact.

While it's been my experience that clients always do better in therapy if they have some kind of spirituality in their lives, it doesn't have to involve going to church or embracing any formal religion. What it does involve is some form of inner reflection or meditative process that occurs on a fairly frequent basis, preferably throughout the day, each and every day, in a way that is integral to daily life.

Over the years, I've worked with many clients who professed to be atheists or agnostics, but who also lived exemplary lives, and behaved in extremely loving, compassionate, and ethical ways with others. In addition, most of these people reported enjoying exercise, hiking, yoga, sketching, or music because these things helped them become calmer and find inner peace.

That's what I'm talking about when I talk about spirituality. The matter is especially important here because in every one of the cases contained in this book, the people involved had that kind of spirituality; moreover, drawing on it proved to be essential for their growth and healing. So, in addition to trying out some of the behavioral interventions these clients made with their children, I hope readers will also take note of the role spirituality plays in parenting, especially in overcoming parent-child problems.

If you find your higher power in church, great, go there. Or maybe you find twelve step meetings bring you closer to whoever your sense of God is. But, if you haven't already tried alternative ways for accessing your spiritual side, I'd like to suggest some of the following activities. None of these are my original thoughts, by the way, but rather suggestions that appear in numerous other self-help books.

1. Build an "altar" in your home and go there to meditate or pray when you feel the need to get centered. Find a quiet corner somewhere where the light appeals to you and place a low table there. Cover it with a cloth you like and place objects on it that have special meaning for you; scented candles or incense, small gifts loved ones have given you, mementos of favorite trips or happy times in your life, and other items that bring you a sense of peace.

2. Overcome "Nature Deficit Disorder," and do something with "Mother Nature" as often as possible. Sit and watch the sunrise or sunset. Take a long walk in the park or the woods. Work in your garden. Do anything you can think of that involves being outdoors, breathing fresh air, noticing your surroundings, or talking to the animals. Oh, and here's the most important part of all: try to do it alone and without any electronic equipment on hand, unless perhaps it's something that plays soft, soothing music. The goal here is to get in touch with your *inner* voice, and that's less likely to happen when you're talking with someone else or readings texts on your cell phone.

3. Volunteer at or just visit a nursing home, homeless shelter or soup kitchen. Jump in and help if they need you. Talk to someone less fortunate than you. Take snacks and sit in the lobby, shooting the breeze with people who come and go.

4. Volunteer at the Humane Society. Handle the most scared and lonely four-legged residents you see there. Shampoo and brush the cats and dogs. Focus on being with the animals rather than chatting with the staff. Donate supplies you know they can use; disinfectant soaps, bleach, paper towels, etc.

5. Go shopping for greeting cards for people you care about, especially people you haven't talked to for a while, or haven't told how you feel about them. Pick out something thoughtful or even mushy if you have something serious you want to say to someone. Or just go for laughs and send something silly to someone who needs cheering up.

6. Practice random acts of kindness. Give someone you know a small gift, something you know they like; a favorite coffee, tea, book, or CD. Do something courteous for someone you don't know; hold the door for them, pick up something they dropped, or hand them some small change when they're short at a checkout line. And don't be discouraged if they don't respond with equal courtesy. This isn't about doing something for others to get something in return, but about spreading good Karma.

7. After you do one of the above activities, write about it in your journal or just sit in silence and think about what happened within you as you had the experience. Ask yourself: how did it feel, what did you learn, and what was the impact of the event on your spirit?

This list could go on forever, but the above suggestions pretty much convey the gist of the matter.

Finally, since this book is about parenting adult children, try sharing your experiences doing these activities with your grown kids. Be prepared for some rolled eyes, sighs, or giggles. Thanks to comedian and now-senator Al Franken's goofy character Stuart Smalley, who recited affirmations to himself in the mirror, as well as other comedians who poke fun at self-help programs, lots of people have come to see self-care steps like the ones above as "hokey." But, that doesn't mean they can't still work for us.

Closing Reflections

One of my criteria for what makes a really good book is feeling like I don't want it to end. With these books, I find myself reading more slowly as I near the last pages, trying to draw out the experience, and keep those fascinating characters alive as long as possible. However, in *writing* previous books, I've never had the experience of not wanting the writing to end. Quite the contrary, I've usually been eager to pack it all up and "put it to bed."

That's not been the case with this book. Right from the beginning it's been a labor of love, probably because I value so much the people whose stories are contained herein, and have really enjoyed collaborating with them on putting their stories together. While that process hasn't always been easy, it *has* always been meaningful and important, for them, they tell me, and for me, as well. I can't count the times one of them has said to me: "It's so *hard* to read these words about myself and my family, but it also makes me so aware of *how far we've all come* from those earlier troubled times."

Like many writers before me, what I found happening as this

project evolved was that the work took on a life of its own. I had always envisioned the book in its basic, present format. But, what I hadn't anticipated was how the collaboration with clients on their stories would become both an extension of and variation on my therapy with them. As we worked together to find just the right wording and phrases to capture their unique personal stories, we probed new depths of the therapeutic relationship, struggling sometimes to avoid hurting feelings or giving offense to each other. The really exciting work began once I was able to convince all of them: "This story is *all about you,* and nothing goes forward that you aren't *totally and completely* comfortable with!" Once we reached that benchmark, I heard some painfully honest, but always right-on-target, feedback about things I needed to change in their narratives. I can truthfully say here that each and every one of the changes clients suggested to me for this work has been made according to their wishes, and that, as a result, the final product is a much better one than anything I might have imagined at its outset.

One of the best ways I can think of to thank and honor those good people is to share some more of their actual comments about the experience of working with me on this book. Here is their input.

Dora Pritchard responded in this way to her first reading of my chapter about her: "I'm sorry, but I just don't see myself here. You've painted me to be such a strong person, but I don't think that's the real me. The real me is a person who deals with overwhelming depression every day of my life. Yes, I go on, because my kids and my husband need me to. But I certainly don't see myself as the brave, resilient person you've made me out to be here. It's almost as if by focusing on my survival skills, you've missed talking about all the pain I've been through and continue to face." Dora asked me to revisit my telling of her story and make clear to readers that the strength she exhibited didn't remove her pain, which I subsequently did.

Similarly, Christy Duncan commented: "Yes, we've coped with and done our best to overcome our daughter's disappearance from our lives, but just because we're survivors doesn't mean we haven't had incredible pain. This is the hardest thing we've ever experienced, no matter how intact we may look on the surface."

In addition, after reading my first draft of their story, Elliot expressed feeling "left out" of the narrative, and understandably so, as Christy pointed out to him: "That's because *I* was the one who went to therapy, *not you*, because you deal with your feelings by staying busy and trying not to think about things that trouble you." Nonetheless, in my final version of their chapter, I added passages dealing more with Elliot's feelings about losing Kelly, in a revision that the Duncans eventually agreed made a much better recounting of their actual story.

I had to chuckle at first at Trent Culbertson's response to reading my chapter about him, but then found myself admiring him anew in a different way, by virtue of the fact that he was so willing to let his story be shared in the hope that it might help and inspire others: "I very much enjoyed reading the items that you sent me that were not about me. I also enjoyed reading the part that was about me, but I have to tell you that I cried my way through it the first time, and had to steel myself to read it again to ensure I didn't miss anything. You have painted a marvelous picture, and the truth that we both know in it resonates strongly. It really hit me hard that it truly was my life and my experiences that you were writing about, and it was hard to relive it and see it all over again. Honestly I wouldn't change anything about it . . . I will be anxious to read the finished product."

Angela Manning, being the true seeker that she is, pored over my chapter about her through several revisions with great attention to detail and with wonderful suggestions: "I'm blown away! I had no idea at first that this chapter was going to be so much about *the real me!* I expected to see a story based on my life with changes that would disguise my identity and focus on the *issues* in my life, but not the *person* that I actually am. Reading this, I realized, 'Oh, my gosh, this really is about *me!*' Having realized that, I went back and looked at it a lot more closely and came up with some changes." Angela did indeed make "some changes," giving me page after page of revisions, all of them wonderful and all of them included in the final copy of her chapter.

Emily Fernandez and Chad Curtis were largely pleased after their first reading, but like all of my parents, also had some changes to suggest. After I submitted my revisions to them, Emily wrote me: "Therapy is about the truth, gotta face it. Our daughter was a real gift to us, for sure. I cried at times, and laughed at times. It's perfect. I am so comforted to know that our story may help other families."

Likewise, Dottie Thomas expressed being glad to be included in a project that might help and inspire others: "I just read the attached excerpts from your book and I could not be more pleased to be represented in this way by you. You really captured the relationship and its roots. It was also very healing and even revealing in some ways to read it from this perspective. Thank you for believing in me, Fred, and for seeing a 'fairy stepmother' in me. That is my goal."

Apparently, without ever intending to I caused a lot of people a lot of tears! Roland Nabb, too talked about his first reading this way: "I love your writing style, but I have to admit I had to read it several times before I got the whole story because I kept crying . . . not in a bad way, but remembering how awful things were with my daughter then, and how wonderful our relationship is now . . . it just moved me so much to think of how far we've come and how much I cherish that relationship now."

Ironically, the most troubled and troubling response I got from any of my contributing parents was also the most valuable, and ultimately the most positive. That was Audrey Talbott's feedback on my first draft of her story: "I felt as if I was portrayed as quite clueless and weak . . . There is really no mention of the immense lengths which I had gone to get our son help, following through on all the 'professional guidance' we had gathered! For families like us, who tried everything for years, I would like to have that acknowledged. It isn't as if I just smiled and said 'yes' to Eric for all those years. He was constantly disciplined, but the demons were bigger than me . . . As for the MD visit . . . I fought with the MD, but he insisted on the med (Klonopin). I feel like that should be shared to show that the system doesn't always guide you the right way . . . I tried *every* day for *years* to get Eric the help he needed . . . This is a really hard story to have lived, be continuing to live and to read about . . ."

After a heartfelt talk with Audrey and a sincere apology on my part for missing the boat so totally on her story, I sent her another version with her suggestions included. Fortunately, that version did a much better job of capturing the essence of her tale, though it, too, needed some tweaking: "Oh *thank you*. My tears on reading this one are for the *reality* of it, not my displeasure. It is beautifully written. The only part I want to review with you is about the MD visit and med . . . but I feel it might be the perfect place to touch upon the 'trust' we have for professionals . . . sometimes proving that our gut feeling was right on . . . continued disappointment and confusion for us. Actually I am enraged by the memory of that care!" These suggestions, too, went into the final copy for this book and on her last reading of her chapter Audrey was totally comfortable with it.

The Rodger's and Hammerstein musical, *The King and I*, includes a song called "Getting to Know You." It opens with the lyrics: "It's a very ancient saying, but a true and honest thought, that if you become a teacher, by your pupils you'll be taught." The same thing is true for therapists and their clients. Over the years, I've worked with hundreds, if not thousands of people from all walks of life, with all kinds of problems, issues, talents, and strengths. Like the parents I worked with on this book, most of these clients have been kind enough to give me good marks for the help I provided them. But I, on the other hand, need to thank them for all the lessons they've taught me, as well as for the commitment to change they brought into our work together, before I even uttered the first words of greeting to them.

In the final analysis, this book is a tribute to all of those brave people who have come to me, wanting my help and support to be better parents to their adult children. Each one of them in their own way got the job done, admirably. My hope is that through reading the stories and suggestions contained here, other parents of adult children will find practical solutions, hope, and even inspiration to overcome whatever parenting challenges they may be facing themselves.

Suggested Discussion Questions for Therapists, Teachers or Other Professionals Working with Clients or Students Who Read This Book

1. What client story or stories do you relate to the most and why?

2. Do you recognize yourself, your own adult children, or your parents anywhere in these pages? If so, how?

3. What ideas, case histories, or other aspects of the book did you find most difficult to relate to, and why?

4. The topics of chemical dependency and codependency come up in several of the case histories contained in this book, as do related topics such as enabling, tough love, and intervention. What is your own personal experience with these topics and issues?

5. The discussion of codependency in this book is a divided one, recognizing the value of the term and all of the self-help literature which has been published about it on the one hand, but also questioning the legitimacy of it on the other hand. What is your personal perspective

about the usefulness of the concept of codependency in your own life, either as a parent of adult children, or an adult child?

6. Grief and loss issues feature prominently in many of the case histories related here. As a parent of adult children, how have grief and loss issues influenced you and your family? How well does the book resonate with your own experience with these issues? If you could suggest changes to the author about these issues, what would you suggest?

7. While all of the therapy techniques illustrated in these case histories are consistent with both national and community norms for sound clinical practice, occasionally they use imaginative processes many therapists feel uncomfortable with, such as the Gestalt empty chair technique," or role-playing *It's a Wonderful Life*, with a suicidal client to help him realize what the world would be like without him. What is your own personal reaction to these creative therapy techniques as you read about them? Would they work for you or your loved ones? Would you feel comfortable with your therapist if she or he tried to use them with you? Why or why not?

8. Many of the parents in these case histories fell into the difficulties they experienced with the best of intentions, wanting only to help their adult child in some way, but then finding they had created a dependency in their child that they couldn't easily escape. How have your

best intentions back-fired on you in your relationships with your adult children? How can you begin to reverse that dynamic? What are the "tough love" choices you may need to make to begin a healthier relationship with your adult child or children?

9. What did you feel as you read this book or thought about it later, remembering its stories and messages? Did you find the ideas and healing strategies contained in it helpful? Was there something else you wanted to hear in it? If so, what was that unmet need? Please write and express yourself to the author at FredSchloemer@aol.com.

BIBLIOGRAPHY

Adams, J. *When Our Grown Kids Disappoint Us.* New York, NY: Free Press, 2003.

Arnett, J. J. (2010). "Oh, Grow Up! Generational Grumbling and the New Life Stage of Emerging Adulthood." *Perspectives on Psychological Science,* 5(1) 89-92.

Beattie, M. *Codependent No More: How to Stop Controlling Others and Start Caring for Yourself.* Center City, MN: Hazelden Foundation, 1987.

Black, C. *It Will Never Happen to Me: Growing Up with Addiction As Youngsters, Adolescents and Adults.* Bainbridge Island, WA: MAC Publishing, 1982.

Campbell, R. and Chapman, G. *Parenting Your Adult Children: How You Can Help Them Achieve Their Full Potential.* Chicago, IL: Northfield Publishing, 1990.

Coleman, J. *When Parents Hurt: Compassionate Strategies When You and Your Grown Child Don't Get Along.* New York, NY: HarperCollins Publishers, 2007.

Conyers, B. *Addict in the Family: Stories of Loss, Hope and Recovery.* Center City, MN: Hazelden, 2003.

Davis, L. *I Thought We'd Never Speak Again: The Road from Estrangement to Reconciliation*. New York, NY: HarperCollins Publishers, 2002.

DeVaus, D. *Letting Go*. New York, NY: Oxford Press, 1994.

Downs, A. *The Velvet Rage: Overcoming the Pain of Growing Up Gay in a Straight Man's World*. Cambridge, MA: DeCapo Lifelong Books, 2005.

Jay, J. and Cline, F. W. *Grandparenting with Love and Logic: Practical Solutions to Today's Grandparenting Challenges*. Golden, CO: The Love & Logic Press, 1994.

Henig, R. M. (2010). "What Is It About 20-Somethings?" *New York Times Magazine*, August 18, 2010.

Hillman, J. *The Dream and the Underworld*. New York, NY: HarperCollins, 1979.

Isay, T. *Becoming Gay: The Journey to Self-Acceptance*. New York, NY: Henry Holt and Company, 1996.

Johnson, Robert. *Owning Your Own Shadow: Understanding the Dark Side of the Psyche*. San Francisco, CA: HarperCollins Publishers, 1991.

Johnson, D. and Johnson, F. *Joining Together: Group Theory and Group Skills*. Needham Heights, MA: Allyn and Bacon, 1994.

Jung, C. G. *Four Archetypes: Mother/Rebirth/Spirit/Trickster*. Princeton, NJ: Princeton University Press, 1959.

Jung, C. G. *Man and His Symbols*. London, England: Aldus Books, 1964.

Kemp, G., Kovatch, S., and Goldstein, A. (2010). "Grand-parenting Tips: Building Great Relationships with Your Grandkids." Online article available at www.helpguide.org/mental/grandparenting.htm.

Kettlehack, G. *Easing the Ache: Recovering from Compulsive Behaviors.* Center City, MN: Hazelden, 1998.

Kinney, J. *Loosening the Grip: A Handbook of Alcohol Information.* Columbus, OH: McGraw-Hill Higher Education, 2009.

Kooden, H. and Flowers, C. *Golden Men: The Power of Gay Mid-life.* New York, NY: Avon Books, 2000.

Kornhaber, A. *The Grandparent Guide: The Definitive Guide to Coping with the Challenges of Modern Grandparenting.* New York, NY: Contemporary Books, 2010.

Leventhal, B. and Lundy, S. *Same-Sex Domestic Violence Strategies for Change.* Thousand Oaks, CA: Sage Publications Inc., 1999.

McKay, M., Davis, M., and Fanning, P. *Messages: The Communication Skills Book.* Oakland, CA: New Harbinger Publications, 1995.

McKay, M., Davis, M., and Fanning, P. *Thoughts and Feelings: Taking Control of Your Moods and Your Life.* Oakland, CA: New Harbinger Publications, 2007.

Nemzoff, R. *Don't Bite Your Tongue: How to Foster Rewarding Relationships with Your Adult Children.* New York, NY: Palgrave Macmillan, 2008.

Reed, R. *Growing Up Gay.* New York, NY: W. W. Norton, 1997.

Steiner, C. *Scripts People Live: Transactional Analysis of Life Scripts*. New York, NY: Grove Press, 1974.

Tobias, A. *The Best Little Boy in the World Grows Up*. New York, NY: Ballantine, 1999.

Vaughan, F. and Walsh, R. *Gifts from a Course in Miracles*. New York, NY: Penguin Putnam Inc., 1983.

Wallace, H. *Family Violence: Legal, Medical and Social Perspectives*. Boston, MA: Pearson Education Inc., 2005.

York, P. & D. and Wachtel, T. *Tough Love*. Garden City, NY: Doubleday & Company, 1982.

Zukav, G. *The Seat of the Soul*. New York, NY: Free Press, 1989.

About the Author

FRED SCHLOEMER is a career psychotherapist and author, as well as a former professor of communication, education, psychology and social work. His previous books include *Just One More Bird*, a self-help book about setting healthy boundaries for children of alcoholics of all ages, and *From a Land in Between: Prose and Poem Tales of Alternative Lives*, an anthology dealing with human diversity. He has published extensively in professional corrections, education, social work and spirituality journals, as well as short stories and poems in numerous anthologies and literary magazines. His monthly Q&A mental health features "Outside the Box" and "Your Peace of Mind" have appeared in the Indianapolis newspaper *The Word* and the Louisville newspaper *The Community Letter* for the last eight years. For more information, visit his website at www.schloemerservices.com.